T0148649

Latinos in Michigan

Discovering the Peoples of Michigan is a series of publications examining the state's rich multicultural heritage. The series makes available an interesting, affordable, and varied collection of books that enables students and lay readers to explore Michigan's ethnic dynamics. A knowledge of the state's rapidly changing multicultural history has far-reaching implications for human relations, education, public policy, and planning. We believe that Discovering the Peoples of Michigan will enhance understanding of the unique contributions that diverse and often unrecognized communities have made to Michigan's history and culture.

Latinos in Michigan

David A. Badillo

Michigan State University Press

East Lansing

♾ The paper used in this publication meets the minimum requirements
of ANSI/NISO Z39.48-1992 (R 1997) (Permanence of Paper)

Michigan State University Press
East Lansing, Michigan 48823-5245

Printed and bound in the United States of America

09 08 07 06 05 04 03 1 2 3 4 5 6 7 8 9 10

LIBRARY OF CONGRESS CATALOGING-IN-PUBLICATION DATA
Badillo, David A.
Latinos in Michigan / David A. Badillo.
p. cm.—(Discovering the peoples of Michigan)
Includes bibliographical references and index.
ISBN 0-87013-645-3 (pbk. : alk. paper)
1. Hispanic Americans—Michigan—History. 2. Hispanic Americans—Michigan—
Social conditions. 3. Immigrants—Michigan—History. 4. Michigan—Ethnic relations.
5. Michigan—Social conditions. I. Title. II. Series.
F575.S75 B33 2002
977.4'00468—dc21
2002153203

Discovering the Peoples of Michigan. The editors wish
to thank the Kellogg Foundation for their generous support.

Cover design by Ariana Grabec-Dingman
Book design by Sharp Des!gns, Inc.

COVER PHOTO: Webster School children (Southwest Detroit Business Association).

Visit Michigan State University Press on the World Wide Web at:
www.msupress.msu.edu

To my late maternal uncles,
Theodore Lit and Alfred Lit,
who taught me much about
the worlds of the immigrant.

ACKNOWLEDGMENTS

I gratefully acknowledge the hospitality of the Center for Chicano-Boricua Studies, Wayne State University, during my year in residence as a visiting professor. Special thanks are due to José Cuello and Javier Garibay.

SERIES ACKNOWLEDGMENTS

Discovering the Peoples of Michigan is a series of publications that resulted from the cooperation and effort of many individuals. The people recognized here are not a complete representation, for the list of contributors is too numerous to mention. However, credit must be given to Jeffrey Bonevich, who worked tirelessly with me on contacting people as well as researching and organizing material.

The initial idea for this project came from Mary Erwin, but I must thank Fred Bohm, director of the Michigan State University Press, for seeing the need for this project, for giving it his strong support, and for making publication possible. Also, the tireless efforts of Keith Widder and Elizabeth Demers, senior editors at Michigan State University Press, were vital in bringing DPOM to fruition.

Otto Feinstein and Germaine Strobel of the Michigan Ethnic Heritage Studies Center patiently and willingly provided names for contributors and constantly gave this project their tireless support. Yvonne Lockwood of the Michigan State University Museum has also suggested and advised contributors.

Many of the maps in the series were prepared by Gregory Anderson at the Geographical Information Center (GIS) at Western Michigan University under the directorship of David Dickason. Additional maps have been contributed by Ellen White.

Other authors and organizations provided comments on other aspects of the work. There are many people that were interviewed by the various authors who will remain anonymous. However, they have enabled the story of their group to be told. Unfortunately, their names are not available, but we are grateful for their cooperation.

Most of all, this work is a tribute to the writers who patiently gave their time to write and share their research findings. Their contributions are noted and appreciated. To them goes most of the gratitude.

ARTHUR W. HELWEG, *Series Co-editor*

Contents

Introduction

The history of Latinos in Michigan is one of cultural diversity, institutional formation, and an ongoing search for leadership in the midst of unique, often intractable circumstances. While facing adversity as rural and urban immigrants, exiles, and citizens, Latinos have contributed culturally, economically, and socially to many important developments in the state's history. They have coalesced into an internally diverse entity as they have engaged in work, residence, and religion, and this essay probes the interrelationship among the various constituent groups. The 2000 U.S. Census indicates that Latinos now comprise about 3 percent (324,000) of Michigan's population, a 61 percent increase since 1990 (in comparison, the state's population as a whole rose only 7 percent in this same time period), spread over much of the state. The proximity of Mexico and the Caribbean—the prime sending areas—and the relatively recent arrival of Latinos set the stage for drama and exhilaration that in its own way rivaled the massive overseas immigration from Europe around the turn of the century.[1]

Latinos have shared a vision of the American Dream—made all the more difficult by the contemporary challenge of cultural assimilation. The complexity of their local struggles, moreover, reflects far-reaching developments on the national stage and suggests the outlines

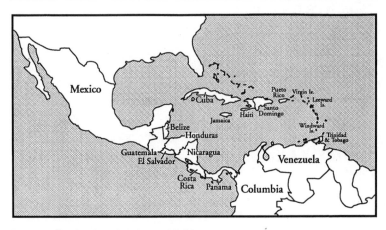

Sources of Latino Immigration to Michigan.

of a common identity. Even the Mexican-origin population (constituting over two-thirds of the present total) has several distinct components. Its presence is greater nationally and regionally than locally; it is generally located throughout the Midwest, whereas the settlement of Puerto Ricans (in the Great Lakes region) and Cubans (primarily urbanites, in Chicago, Cincinnati, and many smaller cities) has happened in more limited areas. While this essay seeks to portray a story that is balanced, geographically and otherwise, developments in the Detroit metropolis have had greater resonance, in that it is the premier urban destination for pioneer migrants and also because it is home to over one-third of the state's Latin American–origin peoples.

Tejanos, Mexican Immigrants, and Mexican American Communities

In the early decades of the twentieth century Mexican Americans in the ranches, towns, and farms of the lower Rio Grande Valley and the Winter Garden area in Texas began expanding as far north as Montana and Minnesota. Large corporations involved in the growing and processing of beet sugar contracted with local growers for the employment of out-of-state seasonal labor, thereby introducing Mexicans into the Michigan economy. The Texas Mexicans, or *tejanos*, Michigan's first Latinos, had lived in Texas for varying periods—sometimes decades, even centuries—because they or their ancestors were born there, because they had crossed the border at some earlier point, or because their arrival predated U.S. annexation of the area in 1845. Their experience as migrant laborers, picking cotton or other crops for low wages, prepared them to work on Michigan farms, at first seasonally and then later permanently. Culturally Mexican and often predominantly Spanish speakers, they readily ventured north to the Great Lakes region and elsewhere in the United States as opportunities developed, and they customarily returned to winter in Texas. Labor recruiters targeted the huge Mexican population residing in San Antonio, the gateway to the Midwest during the 1920s, where railways and highways from El Paso to Brownsville converged. Track work, particularly for the

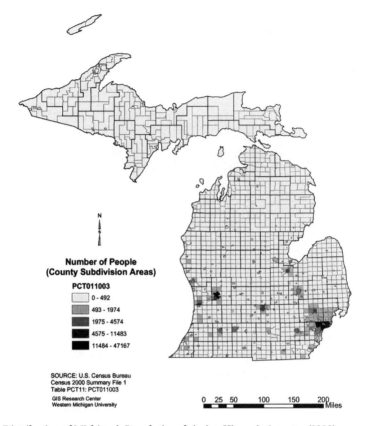

**Number of People
(County Subdivision Areas)**

PCT011003

- 0 - 492
- 493 - 1974
- 1975 - 4574
- 4575 - 11483
- 11484 - 47167

SOURCE: U.S. Census Bureau
Census 2000 Summary File 1
Table PCT11: PCT011003

GIS Research Center
Western Michigan University

0   25   50   100   150   200 Miles

Distribution of Michigan's Population claiming Hispanic Ancestry (1990).

Pennsylvania Railroad Company, also drew many *tejanos* as well as immigrants directly from Mexico to Michigan, where they took jobs in agriculture, increasingly remaining in *el Norte* to work until the following spring, or settling into opportunities in industry.

Tejanos arrived in the Michigan's eastern "thumb" area around 1915 to work in sugar beets, at which time a vacuum had been created in the rural Michigan workforce by the flight of Hungarian and Russian laborers to the cities. Thereafter, the Saginaw-based Michigan Sugar Beet Company brought up thousands of migrants from Texas to replace European-origin immigrants who had "settled out" from the beet fields, often after having accumulated small properties. By the 1920 growing season, almost five thousand Mexicans had arrived in the different parts of southern Michigan, and they soon came to dominate this agricultural sector. These workers, who called themselves *betabeleros*, most of whom had been farmers, sharecroppers, or ranch hands prior to heading north, spearheaded the permanent settlement of Mexican Americans in Michigan. At first they came alone (often having been smuggled into the state aboard covered trucks), but later they arrived with their families, as children and all able-bodied adults effectively served as additional hands to tend the acreage.[2]

Growers and local residents believed that utilizing the family as the basic work unit helped ensure the "reliability" of the seasonal migrants. *Betabeleros* faced many forms of discrimination and exploitation by growers, who treated them as transients, to be unceremoniously returned home after each season—at company expense, if necessary. It was especially feared that they would break their contracts and wander off from the low-paying beet work in isolated communities into cities and towns, competing economically and mixing socially at the end of the season. By the mid-1920s, Michigan's sugar beet work had created what one historian calls an "agricultural proletariat" of almost seven thousand primarily Mexican and *tejano* workers, clearly distinguished by ethnic background, language, and mode of entry from the established residents of rural and urban midwestern communities.[3]

Given the seasonal nature of their migration and the presence of interethnic hostility, the *betabeleros* realized that few opportunities existed for the acquisition of even small farms. For them, therefore, survival often meant stability, and they seized whatever opportunities existed to pursue year-round industrial work. Many remained in beet work for a season and then instead of heading South went to the booming urban centers of southeastern Michigan. As production in Michigan's fruit belt expanded sharply in the 1940s, migrants expanded into the picking of asparagus, cherry, blueberry, and apple crops in western Michigan; they also moved to nearby cities and formed new *colonias*. Undocumented *betabeleros* joined their ranks, in spite of greater immigration restrictions and more tenacious, although always selective (due to the power of the growers' lobby) enforcement.

*Mexican sisters visiting a Mexican migrant worker family in the Archdiocese
(Archives of the Archdiocese of Detroit).*

After 1910 the disruption, violence, and dislocation of society
caused by the Mexican Revolution accelerated the movement of
Mexicans to the Southwest. It also spurred emigration from the interior
states of the *mesa central* (central plateau), primarily Michoacán,
Jalisco, and Guanajuato, to the Midwest. Railroads linked central
Mexico with the Texas border cities of Laredo and El Paso and then connected with Kansas City, allowing for further direct passage. Track
maintenance workers, in particular, obtained easy access to points far-
ther north, and they sometimes established the first *colonias*, or *barrios*
(urban settlements), in midwestern cities. At first, labor agents called
enganchistas recruited workers, but soon family networks precipitated
a chain migration and formed a migrant stream coordinating the needs
of farmers and the Mexican workers. This second group of Latinos in
Michigan entering directly from Mexico had more diverse occupational
backgrounds, with some even skilled as tradesmen and industrial workers, although most were agricultural workers in their home country.

Mexico's church-state crisis, the Cristero Revolt of the mid-1920s, and its attendant disorders, strongly stimulated emigration from Mexico's central plateau to the Great Lakes states, including Michigan. The dynamic factor in the outward flow of population was a peonage system in place on the haciendas that hindered economic development for the populace. Revolutionary violence and economic destabilization, meanwhile, undermined individual security, and the promise of high wages and better opportunities launched many migrants on northward adventures. Most Mexicans expected at first to work in agriculture or for the railroads. Many immigrants arrived in Detroit and other cities only after making preliminary stops in Texas or elsewhere in the Southwest.

By the end of World War I, with the mass production of the automobile and the labor shortages of the period, the number of Mexican

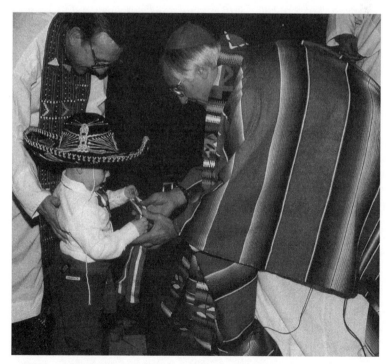

Auxiliary Bishop Thomas Gumbleton (right) *participating in a Cinco de Mayo celebration (Archives of the Archdiocese of Detroit).*

immigrant laborers swelled. Mexicans and a few *tejanos* began filtering in to Saginaw, Flint, Pontiac, and Detroit. Immigrants also found jobs with firms that subcontracted for the major automobile producers, such as Fisher Body, which employed several hundred Mexicans in its southeastern Michigan plants. The first Mexicans came to Flint around 1923, after having been recruited in San Antonio by company agents. Many migrants subsequently took work in industrial jobs developing at General Motors. By the late 1920s, Flint Mexicans had formed a mutual aid society that had a branch for women, as well as a Catholic parish. Detroit soon became the foremost employer of Mexican labor; however, its "Little Mexico," while not as concentrated as the ethnic enclaves of Italians and Poles, was nonetheless a considerably larger and denser *colonia* than that which existed, for example, in Flint, the budding General Motors "company town." Lansing did not develop a solid settlement until the mid-1930s. Saginaw County, in the sugar beet heartland, had attracted Mexican migrants before 1920, but its permanent *colonia* emerged slightly later.[4]

The Mexican colony in Detroit first arose around 1917, when several hundred Mexicans came to the city. This number included over two hundred young men from Mexican engineering and technical schools specifically chosen to work as apprentices on cars, trucks, and tractors in the Highland Park and Fordson plants. After their training they became technicians for fledgling plants and dealerships in Mexico and elsewhere in Latin America. Many remained in Detroit instead, however, where they ascended to higher-income positions. Soon, laborers poured in to replace workmen who had been sent off to fight in World War I. By late 1920, the colony was estimated at eight thousand members, but, facing recession, the colony months later had dwindled to twenty-five hundred persons. As economic conditions improved, Michigan beet companies again called for workers. Ford soon became the largest midwestern employer of Mexicans, with some one thousand workers at the River Rouge plant alone, and other plants and businesses connected with the auto industry soon began to offer good wages and attract Mexican immigrants.[5]

The Motor City, as the nucleus of the nation's fastest-growing metropolitan area, attracted European immigrants and thousands of migrants from the South on its way to becoming the nation's fourth-largest city. Large numbers of African American migrants came to Detroit around 1916 and then again after 1924, when the full effects of restrictive immigration policies had opened the local market to unskilled laborers. Within this urban mosaic some three thousand Mexicans had entered by 1920; this number had increased to fifteen thousand by the late 1920s, according to some unofficial estimates. During these early years Detroit's Mexican population ratio greatly favored males over females, reflecting the prominence of *solos*, or unaccompanied males, coming to work in the assembly lines, foundries, and related areas. High manufacturing wages allowed for the continual sending of remittances back home to help families survive.[6]

Detroit's barrio developed near downtown, close to the factory districts. Characterized by poor housing and restrictive renting practices, it also served to focus cultural life, with a handful of grocery stores, along with pool halls and barbershops (both of which served as social centers) catering to the tastes of Mexicans. Here several distinct waves of migration with differing cultural patterns existed—one involving the offshoots from the agricultural migrant stream (usually *tejanos*) and others consisting of those workers either recruited by labor agents along the border or proceeding directly from the interior. Not all Detroit Mexicans lived within the barrio, which initially lacked well-defined boundaries.

As their numbers increased, a more distinct settlement formed, where, in 1926 several hundred men, mostly transients, lived in boardinghouses, or *casas de asistencia*, which proved to be more economical than renting an apartment or house. These rooming houses usually possessed names of homeland provinces or cities, and they tended to serve persons from the same regions in Mexico. Women helped run the houses, cooking and cleaning, providing a familiar cuisine, and packing lunches for workers as they left in the morning to take the streetcar to the factory. Some individual families also took in relatives and *paisanos* (fellow countrymen) in need of inexpensive dwellings. By the close of the 1920s Mexican women began to expand their workplaces throughout the urban landscape, taking jobs in downtown businesses as packers, cutters, and even machine operators. Second-generation

Mexican American women, especially clerks and office workers, also found work outside of heavy industry. The family, nonetheless, always remained an important institution, as it had in agricultural settings.

The attachment of Detroit Mexicans to their homeland and culture necessitated periodic return travel, causing immigrants to view immigration (albeit often mistakenly) as a temporary phenomenon. Mexican nationals overwhelmingly preferred to retain their citizenship, shunning naturalization out of a sense of nationalism and also for practical reasons, since ties with the consul's office often provided assistance and intervention in times of individual or group crisis, and such services would largely be forfeited with U.S. citizenship. The Mexican government appointed representatives, or consuls general, to help support the sprouting *colonias* in U.S. cities, including one in Detroit. In 1926 this office promoted "cultural retention" as well as allegiance to the homeland through the establishment of La Comisión Honorífica Mexicana, the Mexican Honorary Commission. It supervised and assisted in the observance of *fiestas patrias,* religious and patriotic celebrations, such as the 12 December Feast of Our Lady of Guadalupe and the commemoration of Mexican Independence Day on 16 September. These occasions strengthened the sense of community among immigrants far from home. Movie houses with Latin American films and Spanish-language newspapers reporting both international and local news served a similar purpose.[7]

The collapse of auto manufacturing and the subsequent shutdowns in the early years of the Great Depression triggered mass layoffs in southeastern Michigan, causing thousands of Mexican nationals to lose their jobs. The Civil Works Administration provided employment for a large segment of the Mexican population of Detroit in the winter of 1933 and the spring of 1934. As factory employers began restricting employment to citizens, Mexicans realized that their alien status made them vulnerable to further discrimination. Workers on Detroit track and sewer construction projects similarly found themselves permanently unemployed after municipal authorities required all foreign-born workers to be naturalized. Some turned to railroad track work, while others went on relief, but until the Depression ended relatively few Mexicans took out citizenship papers. Yet, when compared with

Our Lady of Guadalupe Procession (Archives of the Archdiocese of Detroit).

Los Angeles or El Paso, Detroit enjoyed higher, though still meager, naturalization rates, which stood at about 10 percent during the 1930s.[8]

In the early 1930s Mexicans throughout the state experienced massive repatriation, both voluntarily and coerced, from rural and urban
areas. In 1932 more than five thousand Detroit Mexicans returned
across the border, including thirteen hundred offered "free transportation" on rail lines to the border and then to points in the Mexican interior. Various governmental officials opted for this solution, since it was
cheaper to return individuals, at about fifteen dollars per person, than
to sustain them in Michigan with the dwindling relief funds. This dras-
tic measure ignored the rights of the repatriated workers, many of
whom had U.S.-born children. The Welfare Department paid their fares
to the Mexican border, and the Mexican government did the rest. Even

the families of naturalized citizens were urged to repatriate, and the rights of American-born children to citizenship in their native land were explicitly denied or not taken into account. By the end of 1932, fifteen hundred Mexicans had been sent from Michigan, with lesser numbers returning from other nearby states. Repatriates were disappointed with the mode of travel provided and with the facilities offered for adjustment when they arrived in Mexico; land and tools had been promised, but no adequate provisions were made. In any event, this "reverse immigration" throttled the development of small *colonias* throughout Michigan, including those in Port Huron, Saginaw, and Grand Rapids.[9]

Industry, unfortunately, revived very slowly, and by 1936 the number of Mexicans in Detroit had dwindled to twelve hundred, less than 10 percent of the predepression figure; few former employees were sent for before 1939. By then, after the passing of the most violent phases of the Mexican Revolution and its social and economic repercussions, the points of origin of emigrants from Mexico had shifted from the central plateau northward. Thereafter, *norteños*—immigrants from Mexico's northern states, within easy reach of Texas cities—made up the largest group of Mexican nationals traveling to Michigan. Like those from the interior, they were unaccustomed to small town life in the United States, and they sought to work and live in the Detroit metropolis and other large cities. *Tejanos*, also having resumed the cycle of seasonal migration with the revival of economic opportunities, adapted to the isolated, rural areas of Michigan. They often faced discrimination in restaurants, hotels, churches, and other public places, but their greater familiarity with English eased their adjustment into cities after 1940, as it had previously in the fields.[10]

In the late 1930s, Mexican Americans once more sought work in Michigan sugar beet fields, again replacing European workers (who had left the cities in search of agricultural work early in the Depression). The Beet Growers Employers Committee streamlined the process of recruitment, using Mexican American workers to depress wages and undermine future organizing attempts (they reportedly worked for $2 an hour under the union rate), sparking a renewed wave of migration from Texas. The imposition of a higher tariff for imported sugar in 1937 also boosted the domestic industry, until mechanization of the harvest phase of the beets decades later conclusively reduced the need for hand labor. Seasonal migrations north of several thousand *betabeleros* in jalopies, trains, or trucks (generally the same ones used during the season to haul sugar beets to the refinery) became the norm. Although workers remained in Michigan in fulfillment of their contracts for as long as seven or eight months, they actually worked in sugar beets for only seventy-five or eighty days. Therefore, during slack periods, or after the season ended, they often looked for fieldwork in pickles, tomatoes, and onions, as well as in the fruit orchards.[11]

With the defense boom of the 1940s a new influx of Mexicans occurred. By 1943 some four to six thousand Mexican immigrants and their children had been crowded into commercial and factory areas west of Detroit's central business district. In 1942, facing a national labor shortage with the military draft in effect, the United States and Mexico negotiated contract labor agreements under the Bracero Program (which was repeatedly extended until 1964), allowing for the temporary or seasonal use of imported Mexican labor in various sectors of the economy. The War Manpower Commission began the recruitment of railroad hands directly from Mexico for maintenance work on the Michigan Central Line. Many of these midwestern braceros lived in boxcars on railroad property; others worked in agriculture, bunking in abandoned shacks and sheds.[12]

Wartime employment helped bring better jobs to all segments of the population and allowed some mobility for those workers fortunate enough to find work in defense plants. The Mexican *colonia* in Ecorse, outside of Detroit, developed as the Great Lakes Steel Company procured Mexican employees by obtaining certification; a similar process occurred in Pontiac. *Tejanos*, moreover, began moving from agriculture to work in industrial towns, benefiting from the higher wages of unskilled factory jobs and from improved housing in federal projects such as that constructed in Adrian, which constituted a marked improvement over nearby Blissfield's congested migrant camps and substandard facilities. Detroit's relatively real wages, as well as the requirements of many defense factories that first papers be taken out before workers were hired, increased naturalization rates. In general, the more economically successful the immigrant family had become and the more rooted it was in American culture, the greater became the likelihood of naturalization.[13]

Mexico's predominantly rural culture and habitat aided in the preservation of folk culture. The roles of boys and girls in the Mexican immigrant family were considerably altered in Detroit as compared with those in Mexico. Mexican American children, for example, often served as translators for their parents, giving these children greater freedom and responsibility. Similarly, the necessities of industrial employment resulted in lesser parental control over children as they entered factories and engaged in social activities. Intermarriage with Anglo-Americans, moreover, blurred the formation of the kind of fixed caste lines that characterized discrimination against the Mexicans in Texas. Discrimination undeniably occurred at various points, but the immigrant context of the midwestern mosaic more readily muffled ethnic conflicts. These persistent cultural differences, as well as very real socioeconomic fissures, arguably pale, however, before the historic segregation patterns experienced by Michigan's African Americans.

Pioneers of Latino Catholicism

Part of the Latino contribution to Michigan lies in the community's importance to religious institutions, both in lay participation and in the changes the Latino presence brought for archdiocesan and parochial policies on the part of Anglo clergy. Detroit, among the oldest cities in the United States, has played a particularly significant role historically in the implantation of Roman Catholics in the Great Lakes region, a role it has maintained for native-born and immigrant Latinos. The founding of Detroit by Antoine De la Mothe Cadillac in 1701 occurred at a time when France controlled much of the North American interior. The frontier French military post became an outpost of Montreal and the maritime settlements, developing, like them, for the exploitation of the fur trade and the riches of the New World, and trading in brandy, guns, and blankets. As a strategically located commercial city, Detroit depended on long-distance trade and the movement of commercial products such as furs, fish, and minerals to overseas markets. To achieve local stability, Cadillac recommended habitant intermarriage with the indigenous population in surrounding villages, believing that miscegenation would win the Indians' loyalty and further their Christianization. During his tenure as Detroit commandant, which ran from 1701 to 1710, when he was appointed governor of

Louisiana, Cadillac sought missionaries to teach the villagers the French language, to "civilize and humanize them, and to instill into their hearts and their minds the law of religion and of the monarch."[14]

From the 1740s on Detroit grew in prosperity, attracting immigrants from Canada and Irish Catholics from the British colonies. When the British took possession of Detroit in 1760 the city was still largely French Canadian. After the War of 1812 the United States finally took definitive possession of the city and large-scale immigration, mainly from New England and New York, began. Father Gabriel Richard, who served as Detroit's only priest from 1806 to 1821, was born in France to a well-to-do-family. He came to Detroit in 1798, fleeing revolutionary France, and traveled his parish, which extended from Detroit to Mackinac, over Indian trails (at that time it took about seven days just to reach Grand Rapids). Shortly before Richard died in 1832 (he was interred in the original parish seat of St. Anne's), priests of the Redemptorist Order arrived in Detroit, where they soon founded St. Mary's and Holy Redeemer parishes, as well as St. Mary's in Monroe. In the second half of the nineteenth century the Irish and Germans were joined by large numbers of Poles, Hungarians, Czechs, Belgians, Slavs, and Italians, spurring massive church construction projects. As Detroit mushroomed in succeeding decades, Holy Redeemer and the other historic parishes grew apace.[15]

The first Detroit Mexicans worshipped at St. Mary's, the old German parish. As the various Mexican-origin groups mixed it became clear that the Mexican nationals tended to be more involved in organizing cultural institutions. Several mutual aid associations emerged, assuming secular self-help functions as well as reinforcing traditional ties with Mexican Catholicism. El Círculo Mutualista Mexicano formed in 1923 from the Ford-sponsored Latin American Club (which survived in modified form into the 1970s). It produced leaders who founded other social and fraternal groups and helped organize Our Lady of Guadalupe Church, the first exclusively Mexican parish in the Great Lakes region, in 1923. The previous year, some 150 Detroit Mexican families had contributed more than $6,000 for the construction of the new church building. The establishment of the parish had also required support from the hierarchy, which Bishop Michael Gallagher offered when he brought in Father Juan Alanís, an exiled priest from Monterey, in 1920. The founding of Our Lady of Guadalupe occurred during a decade of extensive expansion of the Detroit Archdiocese that saw the creation of some fifty-three new parishes. This church served as a magnet to most Mexicans in the downtown *colonia*, as well as to those becoming absorbed into outlying neighborhoods.[16]

Father Alanís's three Sunday Masses became quite popular. His successor in 1926, the Venezuelan-born Father Luis Castillo, offered two Sunday services, a daily evening Mass, and baptisms. The parish also became somewhat of a shrine for the Mexican patroness, the Virgin of Guadalupe. Father Castillo, however, ran into problems when trying to organize a parochial school. Despite having claimed to have scheduled several hundred children for the opening, few appeared, apparently dissuaded by their parents because of the distance involved in the commute from Mexican residences. One concerned Anglo priest noted that most Mexicans lived several miles from the Mexican church, with children having to be brought to Communion by car.[17] One parishioner lamented that "the poor Mexican has not a ghost of a chance to appreciate his religion," since streetcars and other facilities were not available, urging that the location of "the priest [be] within reasonable distance from his people." The appeal concluded with the warning, "Let us learn a lesson from the Protestants! They are after the Mexicans [and] wisely locate [among them]."[18]

Indeed, Protestant churches had early on begun working among Detroit's Mexican population, a process that intensified in the decades following World War II. One longstanding Baptist congregation, La Primera Iglesia Bautista, paralleled the growth of the *colonia* and remained strong into the early 1960s, when it drew hundreds of Mexican American and Puerto Rican families to Spanish-language sermons. One pastor monitoring the situation in 1939 from the newly created Saginaw Diocese confirmed the threat of competition there: "The various Protestant societies maintain thirty missionaries in this state for the sole purpose of converting the Mexicans to their own particular belief. The Baptists are the most active. All of the Protestant missionaries are well supplied with religious tracts and Bibles that are printed in Spanish."[19] Yet he noted very little progress for all their trouble.

Even without external threats, however, internal rifts persisted in Our Lady of Guadalupe for the remainder of the 1930s, by which time Father Castillo had departed and the parish had begun to dissolve. Castillo had continued run-ins with parishioners based on either homeland conflicts or questions of control over finance and administration. *Cristeros,* fervent Catholics who had suffered during the religious persecutions of the 1920s in Mexico, came to Detroit around 1926, celebrating religious freedom and further boosting attendance at the Mexican church. In 1933, Simón Muñoz and other prominent leaders of Our Lady of Guadalupe petitioned the bishop to remove Father Castillo, holding him responsible for a decline in the number of "good Catholics" in the colony. The notice also mentioned the "disastrous propaganda" started by the Baptist Church in a revival meeting, along with the plotting of "that great Mexican painter, Diego Rivera," who, "talks against the existence of God [and induces] Mexicans to become Communists."[20] Rivera had arrived in Detroit in 1932, accompanied by his wife, artist Frida Kahlo, to work on his mural on automobile workers for the Detroit Institute of the Arts. To ease the plight of the city's jobless factory workers, he had helped organize the Liga Mexicana de Obreros y Campesinos (Mexican Workers and Peasants League) to finance and encourage humane treatment of repatriates. His other, more controversial, activities—such as lectures on the evils of capitalism and the promise of socialism—sparked harsh criticism and outrage from many, including the Mexican laity.

With Mexican immigration to the Midwest in reverse during the 1930s, Anglo-American and European-origin Catholic clergy acted to protect Mexicans from perceived spiritual decline. Cardinal Edward F. Mooney, who presided over the Detroit Archdiocese from 1937 to 1958, encouraged the integration of Latinos within established parishes. With the radical curtailing of immigration after World War I, ethnic parishes were in the process of Americanization, a process Mooney sought to continue by proposing Mexican participation in "American" Catholic parish organizations. Several Detroit churches, reflecting local demographic changes, began to receive Spanish-speaking newcomers as parishioners beginning in the 1940s, a process that has continued, with repeated modifications, to the present.[21]

Community Redevelopment in Southwest Detroit

In 1989, the Southwest Detroit Business Association (SDBA) joined the Hubbard-Richard Community Council to form the Mexicantown Community Development Corporation (MCDC), a nonprofit corporation. Securing state funds, the organization identified issues that impeded retail growth in the area, such as lack of parking, security, and amenities. Local community residents sought to revitalize their neighborhood without sacrificing the landscape. The construction of Fiesta Gardens at Bagley and 21st Street, completed in 1991, was the first phase of a plan developed by MCDC to revitalize the section of Bagley just east of the I-75 freeway. The courtyard plaza, featuring a Spanish-style archway, ornamental iron and brickwork, and colorful landscaping, is used for holding special ceremonies, listening to music, or simply taking a break from everyday life.

Plans for a community development project grew out of shared concerns over the lack of commercial investments along Bagley. MCDC has focused on landscape improvements and the need to increase the consumer base in the area so that any new development would not take customers from existing businesses. Among their many redevelopment activities, SDBA offers "Shop-Your-Block" fairs to stimulate commerce, while MCDC sponsors fiestas that showcase the rich ethnic heritage of the Mexicantown area, spotlighting Michigan Latino artists, craftsmen, retailers, and importers of goods from Latin America. The Bagley Housing Association, near historic St. Anne Church, designed and built twenty-two modest new frame houses that mesh well with the neighborhood's Victorian cottages. They plan to add twenty-three more, plus a complex of senior citizen condominiums.

Every September, Casa de Unidad, a nonprofit arts and media organization, sponsors the Unity in the Community Festival at Clark Park. Its purpose is to identify, develop, and preserve the Latino/Hispanic Cultural Heritage of southwest Detroit and to create an awareness of this heritage among all citizens within southeastern Michigan. This organization also conducts workshops, offers technical assistance for artists for concerts and performances, and publishes literary works and collections and a statewide Hispanic Arts Directory. Other Detroit institutions involved with Latino community issues include the Detroit Council of the Arts, La Sed Youth Center, Latino Family Services Youth Center, Roberto Clemente Youth Center, and Wayne State University's Center for Chicano-Boricua Studies.

Although several other churches in southeastern Michigan and throughout the state also have experienced influxes, three parishes—Holy Trinity, St. Anne, and Holy Redeemer in the southwest Detroit barrio—have, in varying degrees, pioneered in the care of Latino families. In 1943 Father Clement Kern, after studying in Mexico, came to Holy Trinity Church, where he served as pastor throughout the 1950s and 1960s, becoming somewhat of a patriarch of the area's Latino community. He started evening English-language classes in the parish school, acted as an advocate against the exploitation of Mexican braceros, and helped organize Casa María, a social work agency providing assistance to the needy. Father Kern also encouraged all his parishioners to engage the surrounding community in celebrations such as the Feast of Our Lady of Guadalupe and related endeavors. One Mexican American woman long active in church affairs noted that parishioners "all worked very hard," in accord with Father Kern's leadership, "[branching out] to different parishes each year [wherever] there were Spanish-speaking people."[22]

Father Kern incorporated the struggle for social justice and the rights of workers into his religious work as pastor from 1943 to 1977, a time when Mexican families moved gradually along Michigan Avenue to the area around Holy Trinity Church in the section of Detroit known as Corktown. The construction of the Lodge Expressway immediately east of the church and the razing of many city blocks directly in front of the church have meant that many of the Mexicans were eventually forced to seek housing elsewhere. In the 1960s he opposed the extension of the Bracero Program and supported César Chávez very early in the farm workers movement, building coalitions between the church and the government for community development. Kern also trained his associates, Latino and non-Latino alike, for work with the region's newest migrants.[23]

With the disappearance of housing in the Holy Trinity area, St. Anne Church in the Bagley Avenue neighborhood came to play a major role in attempting to organize the Mexican colony into a community. After World War I, the French gradually moved away from the area, while Irish and other ethnic groups moved in, and since about 1940 St. Anne's has also served Mexicans. The first Spanish sermon for adults

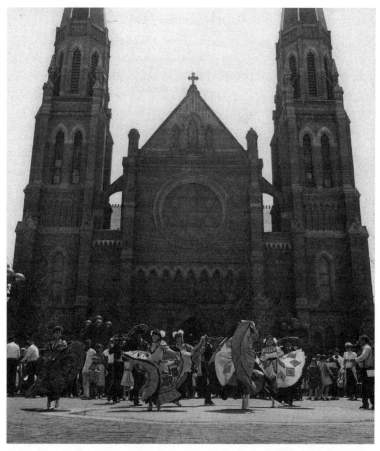

Celebration in front of St. Anne Church (Archives of the Archdiocese of Detroit).

was reportedly held in a separate chapel in 1946; youngsters, meanwhile, attended the English mass in the main church with a mixed
American group. Many parishioners, however, believed that such discriminatory treatment signified a rejection of their culture, and one lay
group, the Caballeros Católicos, in the 1950s requested permanent
Spanish-speaking priests. It also urged the observance of Mexico's
patroness, as had occurred in the old Guadalupe church. By the 1960s,
sheer force of numbers and the changing trends of religiosity in the
wake of the Second Vatican Council dictated that Spanish sermons be

used in the main chapel, in effect making it a national parish (although non-Mexican Latinos also composed part of the ethnic mix). Incoming Puerto Ricans also gravitated to St. Anne's and other barrio churches, developing strong affiliations with their religious clubs. In the 1960s about 500 of St. Anne's 920 families were of Mexican background, and over half of the 250 youngsters in the parish elementary school were Spanish-speaking.

Outside of regional capital cities in their homeland, the Mexican people have generally had little opportunity for formal religious instruction because of the lack of priests in Mexico, a historical circumstance that predated the revolution. Since the Mexican family has been quite mobile, moreover, it has been difficult to establish separate parishes for them in the Midwest. Between 1941 and 1946, Father James Barrett served in a Mexican ministry on the southwest side of Detroit, using the chapel behind St. Anne Church as a "Spanish Parish Church" while fashioning changes in church life that required active and concerned parishioners. At the rear of the chapel, Father Barrett set up a miniature lending library of Spanish religious books; distributed a monthly bulletin, "La Voz Católica Mexicana," throughout the community; and established the Mexican American Youth Association to promote youth activities. After a decades-long stint in Texas, Father Barrett returned to Detroit in the late 1960s and became a member of an ecclesial team commissioned by the archdiocese to strengthen pastoral outreach to Latinos.[24]

The Michigan Avenue-Bagley area was the nucleus of the Mexican colony from the 1920s through the 1940s. Thereafter, the zone from Holy Trinity Church several miles westward along Vernor Highway became lined with Mexican stores; the somewhat improved housing in this area also allowed for some socioeconomic mobility. In the late 1940s and the 1950s, when new expressway construction forced many Mexicans out of Holy Trinity, a number of them moved further southwest, joining Holy Redeemer Parish, which has remained a stronghold for Spanish-speaking Catholics, attracting adherents from throughout the city and even the suburbs. Holy Redeemer, which originally served primarily Hungarian and Polish families who settled nearby in Detroit's lower west side at the turn of the century, came to occupy a central location in the heart of the barrio. It began serving Mexican immigrants drifting into its boundaries around 1950, but relegated Spanish services to the church basement until 1961. A Guadalupe Society met monthly for religious services and in preparation for the annual December celebration, adapting the church's wide range of ceremonies and practices to the Latino presence. The entrance of more Mexican children into the parish elementary school reflected the continued archdiocesan commitment to Americanization and assimilation and, increasingly, the declining effectiveness of barrio public schools.

Puerto Ricans, Cubans, and Other Latinos

Michigan Mexicans generally enjoyed more rapid assimilation of American culture than was possible in the Southwest. Nonetheless, prevailing prejudices since the 1920s portrayed Mexicans and Mexican Americans in Michigan, particularly those in agriculture, as cheap, docile, and temporary laborers to be forgotten when no longer needed. These sentiments were readily transferred to the first Caribbean contingent of Latinos—the Puerto Ricans. Technically considered migrants rather than immigrants because of U.S. citizenship bestowed upon that island territory (now called a commonwealth) in 1917, Puerto Ricans took advantage of the increased demand for seasonal workers by corporate agricultural interests to enter the state in large numbers in the years immediately following World War II. A handful had filtered in earlier via New York and other points. In 1947 and 1948 the Puerto Rican Department of Labor approved contracts guaranteeing suitable working conditions, insurance, and travel, thereby allowing the introduction to the mainland of thousands every season. They either worked on farms in southeastern Michigan or fanned out across the state, generally from June to November, supplementing the work of *tejanos* and Mexicans. U.S. labor agents aggressively recruited unskilled rural villagers through intensive radio advertising campaigns on the   25 island and then flew them north on sometimes perilous journeys aboard charter airplanes. Several midwestern companies advertised in newspapers and over the radio on the island; word of mouth from friends and relatives already on the mainland attracted others.[25]

Puerto Ricans constituted an important and distinguishable component of Spanish-speaking communities after World War II. Very little migration occurred during the Depression or the World War II era. Beginning in the late 1940s, however, Governor Luis Munoz Marín attempted to transform the island's stagnant agrarian economy by attracting U.S. investment to nascent industries. About one-third of the island's labor force, having been displaced from its land and traditional way of life, journeyed north between 1945 and 1960. Puerto Ricans came to the United States in greatest concentrations during the 1950s, a time when the midwestern economy needed entry-level workers. They entered several labor markets, concentrating in Chicago, Milwaukee, and Detroit but extending also along the migrant stream. Puerto Ricans in the Great Lakes states became part of mixed-origin Latino communities. Like Mexican braceros, they first came to the Midwest in large numbers as contract workers, but their U.S. citizenship has allowed them greater ease of movement to and from their homeland.[26]

The recruiting of Puerto Rico agricultural workers involved arrangements between the beet companies and charter airlines. In the fall of 1950, during the slack season in the island's sugar cane industry, planes carrying fifty to sixty passengers each brought over two thousand migrants to Michigan in the space of two weeks for the harvest. This Saginaw Valley airlift was huge in numbers, if not in lasting impact. Workers were paid fifty-five cents per hour, and there were allegations of numerous contract violations and mistreatment by the Michigan Sugar Company that prompted calls for an official investigation. Soon after, this ill-fated venture ended, and Puerto Ricans left the sugar beet district. During the 1950s and 1960s, however, thousands of migrants worked the harvests in Florida and in the Northeast.[27]

Puerto Rican migrants promptly discovered that working conditions on the mainland failed to live up to the favorable depictions of the recruiting agencies. Many of the Saginaw migrants quickly tired of the poor housing, low pay, and bitter cold and left agricultural work after their contracts expired. Making their way to Detroit, they often settled in the very same blocks of the barrio as the Mexicans, forming a culturally diverse Latino neighborhood with an interesting array of Latino businesses developing alongside one another, most using Spanish as the lingua franca. Unlike the pattern in Chicago, however, no separate Puerto Rican area emerged in Detroit.[28]

As the solos sent for their families, direct migration began to take place with neighboring communities in the Detroit metropolitan area. Many Puerto Ricans came to work in industrial and service jobs in Pontiac and Flint, where, in a manner similar to that of the Mexican Americans, they dispersed widely and mixed with the general population. A sense of ethnic solidarity has persisted, nevertheless, as evidenced by annual celebrations of Puerto Rican heritage. A strong Afro-Caribbean culture, particularly evident in salsa music and Latin dance, has marked the introduction of the "Puerto Rican spirit" into Michigan. In 1980, twelve thousand Puerto Ricans represented about 8 percent of the state's Latino population, with the proportion in southeastern Michigan approaching 10 percent. Declining economic opportunities in heavy industry, along with other factors in the homeland and in *colonias* elsewhere in the United States, have led to a decline in migration in recent decades, although considerable back-and-forth movement among the migrants for social as well as economic reasons continues.

The arrival of Puerto Ricans in Detroit, as elsewhere, sparked confusion and prompted concern among the clergy. Father Kern, who eased their settlement in the barrio, remembered working "very hard winning friends" among the disillusioned newcomers as pastor of Holy Trinity. Puerto Ricans, according to Kern, were less well versed in formal Catholicism even than Mexicans: "They simply do not come [to Mass]. Yet that does not keep them from calling us if they get in any trouble, car accident or police trouble." He helped procure jobs for some five hundred of the migrants "in every kind of work." With the onset of the first winter, the majority of the Puerto Ricans went back to their homeland, but over one hundred remained; they soon began to send for their families, and "some dozen or more have bought houses in and out of the colony." As to their patterns of religious devotion, "The

majority has had very little contact with the Church by way of instruction. All seem to feel friendly towards it, knowing very little about its
doctrine or morals. Most of them are [now] in Steel and in heavy industries and they are valuable workers." Although "frugal fellows, saving
their money for the most part," they had little experience with banks;
thus the parish credit union offered them some degree of financial
security. "They are cherished by all good management in town here and
have a good general name." Kern sought to enhance their religious and
moral standing as well.[29]

Cubans offer yet another historical dimension to Michigan's Latino
experience. Between 1961 and 1971 the federally sponsored Cuban
Refugee Center in Miami, along with several religious and voluntary
organizations and innumerable individual and family sponsors
throughout the country, helped resettle several hundred thousand
refugees from the Cuban Revolution. During these years the federal
government resettled Cubans outside of South Florida, hastening their
economic independence while easing the housing and employment
conditions of those remaining in Miami, isolating Cuban families yet
removing them from incipient urban barrios. The resettlement process
targeted professionals, providing certification and licensing for doctors, lawyers, university professors, and teachers. This program sought
to alleviate the growing congestion of Miami and offer humanitarian
aid. Wherever they were relocated, most of the Cubans remained
staunchly anti-Castro. The exile influx included a large number of professionals in the early 1960s, coming primarily from the upper strata of
pre-Revolutionary society, usually originating in one of the larger cities,
such as Havana or Santiago. The composition shifted downward with
time, becoming increasingly representative of Cuban society as a
whole. The educated, professional class, nonetheless, had been drained
following revolutionary edicts affecting both urban and agricultural
sectors.

Many Cubans sought to remain in Miami indefinitely, and some
required public assistance, which was financed by the federal government. Most of the refugees, however, worked below their skill levels,
often in marginal or seasonal positions. For several years after Fidel
Castro suspended commercial air flights from Cuba following the

Cuban Missile Crisis in October 1962, relatively few new Cuban refugees arrived in the United States. During that interlude the resettlement of tens of thousands of refugees occurred in order to take some of the burden off of Miami. In September 1965, Castro permitted unrestricted departure of all dissatisfied Cubans whose exiled relatives came to transport them to Florida. In December 1965, under a negotiated "Memorandum of Understanding," the United States immediately initiated an airlift to Miami. These ongoing "freedom flights" lasted until 1973, bringing almost three hundred thousand Cubans to the United States, where they received special entrant status. The early Cuban exodus consisted largely of the upper class, whose experience and access to financing provided avenues for accumulating capital. Initially, refugees experienced difficulty in finding jobs. With time, however, they contributed to the economic revitalization of the areas in which they settled or resettled. Ethnic solidarity and nationalism based on a strong anti-Castro ideology accompanied Cubans as they dispersed nationally, caught up squarely in the midst of U.S. cold war diplomacy.[30]

Congress favored resettlement as a solution to the concentration of exiles in Miami, but it also saw it as a linchpin in cold war diplomacy. Asylum for the victims of oppression offered the chance to rebuild lives until conditions permitted a return to their homeland, which was thought to be imminent by many, or, for those who wished it, U.S. citizenship became an option. The humane treatment of the Cubans in such a broad stage proved essential for democracies. The giving of effective asylum would also help influence a restructured, post-Castro Cuba and limit the spread of communism, especially in Latin America, and thus preclude additional refugee flows that would further strain the resources of the U.S. treasury. Toward these ends, the federal government contributed hundreds of millions in funds annually to the Cuban refugee program. The pursuit of the self-sufficiency of the Cuban exiles, on a voluntary basis, therefore, became a key piece of global security. With the lull in the influx, authorities had time to develop deliberate methods of resettlement and training, and Catholic and Protestant agencies agreed to work jointly to fill sponsorships. The Church World Service was particularly helpful in providing Protestant sponsors to resettle Cubans in Michigan.[31]

Some forty-five different Michigan communities successfully arranged homes and jobs for over 750 Cuban refugees (ranking it thirteenth among the states in the number of refugees resettled). New York City had the largest number of resettled Cuban refugees, followed by New Jersey. While lawyers and dentists were difficult to retrain, nearly 1,200 doctors were put through a retraining program and sent out into the communities under the guidance of U.S. doctors, where they eventually took state examinations. There were also over three thousand unaccompanied children in thirty-nine different states, whose reunion with their parents was impeded by the inability of the latter to leave Cuba or to enter from other countries, such as Spain and Mexico. By mid-1963 the Catholic Relief Services had resettled some 1,800 Cuban refugees in the Chicago area, some 238 in Detroit, 12 in Grand Rapids, 114 in Lansing, and 14 in Saginaw. Another 10,000 went to New York, 8,000 to Newark, 3,500 to Puerto Rico, and 2,300 to Los Angeles. Resettlement clearly favored the cities, where local conditions, as well as social and political climates, varied greatly, and the exiles generally assimilated rapidly. The case of the small towns, however, highlights aspects of their adjustment that might otherwise remain unexamined.[32]

The reception of the exiles by the larger community during the early years of their immigration not only differs from that experienced by the Mexican Americans, Puerto Ricans, and other Latinos. It is unique in the annals of U.S. immigrant history, since the refugees were the first to come directly from their home country. Moreover, the resettlement program that dispersed them widely constituted an intensive cooperative effort between government and religious organizations administered by the Department of Health, Education, and Welfare. By late 1963, when U.S. Senate Judiciary Committee hearings on resettlement were held in Grand Rapids, about 170,000 Cubans had registered at Miami's Refugee Center and some 68,000 were already resettled in over 1,500 communities throughout the country. The resettlement program proved to be a successful one but, as the testimonies revealed, both the refugees and the welcoming communities faced many challenges, and each had to make significant contributions to the welfare of the other. The head of the Senate subcommittee formed to investigate problems of the Cuban refugees, Philip Hart, noted that the voluntary agencies and their many individual contributors determined the quality of the U.S. response. He viewed the key reasons for supporting resettlement as the need to highlight the virtues of a democratic society, the need to enhance the U.S. reputation for humane treatment and moral leadership internationally, and the need to positively influence "the kind of Cuban Government and society which will follow Castro."[33]

In the 1960s Michigan employed the third-largest number of migrants nationwide, as continued patterns of rural to urban settling out-fed the expansion of Mexican American *colonias* such as Grand Rapids, Muskegon, and Holland, where Cubans had filtered in. Grand Rapids and nearby communities in western Michigan hosting the exiles chronicled some of their anecdotal impressions at the hearings. The mayor of Holland, Michigan, noted that several Christian Reformed Church congregations sponsored the three families in his city. One exile found work at the town's wooden shoe factory, attended church regularly, and became actively engaged in the mission program with the Mexican migrants. Another believed that the resettlement of refugees would be beneficial by giving Americans a chance to learn more about events in Cuba and the persecution of the communist regime.[34] Another refugee exile explained, "Coming from a tropical country [we may never adapt to Michigan weather, but] it's better to [suffer] the 'white monster' . . . than the monster that we have in Cuba."[35]

Observers noted that Cubans had been given preferential treatment in their orientation. The Grand Rapids chamber of commerce assisted in securing employment for about twenty of the refugees with several manufacturing firms, and a Christian school enrolled thirty Cuban children.[36] The mayor called the Cuban refugees to his city "exemplary citizens" who "set a pattern for the rest of us who have slowed up somewhat [and gotten] soft."[37] In Muskegon, refugee families sponsored by several Christian Reformed Churches adapted successfully, despite the initial apprehensions of townspeople that Cubans would compete for jobs. The families were provided good housing, fully furnished through donations by church members, their children were placed in local Christian schools, and the wives were invited to participate in church functions. Former missionaries to

Latin America and a well-known Cuban refugee from Grand Rapids
assisted at church services.

In several cases the exiles left their new communities despite lav-
ish attention. At least one family chose to move in with relatives in New
York, and it became clear that some of the urban exiles found rural life
in Michigan almost unbearable. Moreover, skilled workers were soon
restless with jobs as common laborers. One exile, a factory manager in
Cuba, worked as a Spanish-speaking supervisor for a largely Mexican
workforce on a poultry and hog farm. Local observers thought highly of
the refugees and noted that their status clearly differed from that of the
Mexican migrants, who were often forced to sacrifice their children's
education in the pursuit of a living in agriculture, causing hardships
right from the beginning. Cubans, by contrast, customarily graduated
from high school, and many went on to complete a university education. Despite initial language difficulties, their permanence in the communities in which they settled served them well.[38]

The juxtaposition of incoming Cubans with the long-standing
Mexican situation is instructive. In the 1940s a few Mexican Americans
who came to the area as migrant farm laborers began dropping from
the stream, settling in Holland and its environs and entering the local
labor market. As Holland welcomed industry in the 1950s it also opened
somewhat widely the doors for migrant dropouts. More jobs for the
unskilled and semiskilled enticed greater numbers of farm workers into
the shops and plants. Soon there was a critical mass of Mexican
Americans, which itself attracted relatives and friends into the community. By 1970, the close to four thousand Latinos in the area included
a prominent Mexican American population as well as a group of thirty
displaced Cuban refugee families and a few Puerto Ricans. The town's
surrounding population of approximately fifty thousand remained
dominated culturally by Reformed Protestants of Dutch descent, a religious homogeneity that set the area apart somewhat from other cities
hosting dropouts from the migrant stream.

The establishment of a separate Hispanic Christian Reformed
Church in Holland evidenced a reluctance or inability fully to integrate
Latinos, as well as an urge to evangelize. In the early years of migrants
settling out, the Catholic Church maintained but later abandoned a

separate chapel for the Spanish-speaking Mexicans and Mexican Americans, many of whom worked for the Heinz Company. Although Cuban society in Holland became close-knit, Cubans sought to be assimilated as quickly as possible into the American middle class and to assume a status comparable to what they had known in the past. Their children were Americanized, and they lost touch with their cultural roots. Only one Catholic Church served a four-hundred-square-mile parish, along with six Baptist churches, twenty-two Reformed Churches of America, and twenty-four Christian Reformed Churches. In Grand Rapids, Cubans were also seen as being aloof from other Latinos in their community.[39]

By the early 1970s, almost 3,000 Cubans had resettled in more than seventy Michigan localities—a remarkably wide distribution within a short period of time. They rapidly assimilated, whether in central cities or in the suburban fringe. As it soon became clear that the communist regime would not readily fall—and that the exiles, as they saw themselves, might remain indefinitely on the mainland—Michigan Cubans characteristically set about establishing small businesses, employing fellow exiles where possible. Some families returned to Miami and other South Florida communities in the 1970s; by 1980, nonetheless, some 4,000 Cubans and Cuban Americans lived in Michigan. During the 1970s many Cubans returned from other areas of the country, joining their Miami compatriots in Dade County's southwestern suburbs and further north in Broward and Palm Beach counties. In 1980 the sudden, controversial Mariel Boatlift sparked a new influx that brought hundreds of Cuban refugees to Michigan, including a greater percentage of small-town residents and Afro-Cubans. Almost 125,000 persons departed from the port of Mariel, and a large proportion ultimately settled in South Florida. Makeshift resettlement developed to ease the burden on Miami, and after initial processing in military bases and other facilities, many of these *marielitos* faced relocation—including to Detroit and other areas with an established Cuban-American presence. Many of them filtered into the southwest Detroit barrio and found themselves competing economically with other Latinos in a declining industrial job market. They bore the added burden of being labeled "undesirable." Their ambivalent reception, moreover, contrasted greatly with that given the earlier, wealthier, and often lighter-complexioned émigrés who arrived during the 1960s.[40]

The Cubans, an important component of the Latino experience, represent a traditional "success story," a group enjoying comparatively high socioeconomic levels. They are also older, and their children more inclined toward exogamy, or intermarriage with non-Latinos, than Mexican Americans and Puerto Ricans (although these two groups intermarry in southwest Detroit). Cubans more often occupy the ranks of skilled and professional workers; Mexicans and Puerto Ricans are characteristically unskilled or semiskilled. Cuban households have tended to be the most affluent among Latinos, with those of Puerto Ricans the most economically disadvantaged. The favorable reception offered Cubans by the U.S. government, as well as their previous education, professional training, and experience in the homeland undoubtedly spurred their adaptation. Their circumstances illuminate the vast internal complexity of the Latino community in America as well as its linkages to hemispheric and even global developments.[41]

Detroit Latinos arrive from elsewhere in Michigan, from Texas and the Southwest, and from the Caribbean and elsewhere in Latin America. After World War II, Puerto Rican migrants settled in the southwest Detroit community, where the Spanish-speaking population had swelled with the jobs provided by increased wartime and postwar production. Southwest Detroit, Michigan's largest barrio, has long served as an entry point for Mexican and Caribbean culture. In the late 1980s it also became a sanctuary for Central American refugees and exiles awaiting entry into Canada after fleeing political, religious, or other types of persecution, as well economic devastation, particularly in El Salvador and Guatemala. Southwest Detroit, unlike East Los Angeles, for example, still contains a large number of non-Latino residents, including Poles, Lebanese, and others.

When considering the newer Latino groups, such as Guatemalans, Salvadorans, and others, the issue of immigrant versus refugee status often surfaces. Refugees from the countries of Central America have lived in the United States for many years. Unprecedented regional turmoil and upheaval, however, followed the *Sandinista* victory in the Nicaraguan Revolution of 1979. The counterinsurgency tactics of the military regimes of El Salvador and Guatemala spurred a steady stream of refugees into Mexico and then the United States. If forced to return, many refugees would have faced certain punishment from authorities in their home countries. Catholic and Protestant clergy and laity banded together to carry forth a sanctuary movement, designating local churches as "safe havens." Churches supported individual petitions for political asylum. Detroit served as a way station for many refugees, Salvadorans and Guatemalans especially, who later crossed over into Windsor, Canada.[42]

Immigrants from the countries of South America have contributed small but significant numbers of minorities to Michigan's population. As elsewhere, the Colombians, Ecuadorians, and Peruvians who predominate among the immigrants generally have attained higher levels of education and enjoy higher incomes. Their urban origins have exposed them to standards of living and systems of technology that often compare quite favorably with those of the United States. They are also more geographically dispersed within the metropolis, often living apart from inner city Mexican Americans and Puerto Ricans. Fannie Fabares, a Colombian woman quite familiar with the cultural landscape of the South Americans, who number more than one-fourth of the world's Roman Catholics, directs the Hispanic ministry in the Diocese of Kalamazoo. She believes that Latinos may become more conservative in the United States than in their native countries, because "they do not have as many possibilities to express and live their popular religiosity" as they conform to the circumstances of the local parishes. Churches in western Michigan celebrate distinctive holidays for their parishioners in observance of Peruvian, Venezuelan, Colombian, and Argentinian feast days.[43]

As was the case with other Latino groups, South American priests and religious rarely migrated north with their parishioners. Those who have, however, often have found themselves in leadership positions within their dioceses and on a national level within the church, indicating the value that the U.S. hierarchy places both on their experience and on the desirability of continued outreach to Latino parishioners. South and Central Americans often speak out for justice and solidarity, and many have worked in their homelands through ecclesiastical base communities (*comunidades de base*) to pursue these tenets of Liberation Theology, devoting themselves to the poor, the immigrants, and the refugees, especially those persecuted by autocratic regimes. South American immigrants generally speak Spanish at home and teach their children the language from birth. They believe that the church should offer a bilingual ministry that integrates children, youth, and adults across generations while maintaining aspects of the ancestral culture. It is in line with the goal of many Mexican American and Puerto Rican church activists to facilitate the birth of new culture.[44]

Rise of Rural and Urban Activism

The post–World War II decades brought about a rising awareness among Mexican Americans nationally of the need for collective mobilization to achieve full civil rights. One organization, the League of United Latin American Citizens (LULAC), had been active in Texas since 1929 in seeking equality regarding education, housing, and other issues. During the war the Fair Employment Practices Committee launched investigations regarding discriminatory hiring practices in defense-related industries in the Southwest. Returning Mexican American veterans formed the G.I. Forum to alleviate discriminatory treatment in southwestern institutions. Many areas in the public and private sector, however, particularly in the Midwest, remained retrograde in their treatment of Mexican Americans. By the 1960s a radical generation espoused the cause of *La Causa*, the civil rights cause for Chicanos (the name that activists adopted, replacing Mexican Americans). A key element of the Chicano Movement was support for the campaign to organize farm workers, which developed a midwestern component. Due to the unique regional mix, La Causa reached out to all Latino groups, although nationalistic tendencies and identities have remained separate.

The Catholic Church also entered a more activist phase during the mid-1940s, with the formation of the Bishops' Committee for the Spanish-Speaking (BCSS), which sought to call attention to aspects of urban and rural poverty. During the ensuing two decades the BCSS adopted a new pastoral and social consciousness as concerned rural migrants and, to a lesser extent, barrio residents. The plight of the migrants, though largely hidden from public view, became increasingly visible as crusading journalists such as Carey McWilliams and other reformers chronicled the abuses they faced in their journeys across regions and borders. The concentration of agricultural land and wealth in fewer and fewer hands unfairly subjected Mexican American workers to low wages and unpleasant working conditions, while undermining educational opportunities and otherwise blocking entry of whole segments of the population into the middle class.

The conveying of seasonal labor from Texas to Michigan during the 1940s entailed many such untidy elements, as Spanish-speaking agents for sugar companies, usually Mexican Americans, rode the trains heading out of San Antonio and Fort Worth to convince passengers to sign up with them. Transportation was arduous for the five-day rail journey, with stops in St. Louis and Chicago, and even more unpleasant for those who went by truck. San Antonio residents destined for the fields of Blissfield, Michigan, for instance, were packed together in June 1941 in a crowded vehicle, traveling nonstop for three days and two nights. After the migrants arrived they were usually housed in shacks with no plumbing or electricity, with their expenses collected from wages at company stores. At the end of the season the workers had just enough money to get back to Texas on their own, with no wage at all guaranteed, should the crops be poor or a drought occur. In fact, when beet work was slow, the migrants had to seek day labor elsewhere, harvesting potatoes, cucumbers, beans, and other crops. The annual pilgrimage northward customarily tapered off in the summer months, and patterns of influx and outflow remained erratic throughout the year.[45]

By the early 1950s over 50,000 out-of-state farm workers were coming to Michigan annually, mostly from Texas. There also began an importation of over 2,000 Mexican nationals, the braceros. The Michigan State Employment Service estimated that about 10,000 Spanish-speaking migrants came annually into the Saginaw region during the sugar-beet season. Many of them departed in July to work the cherry crop around the Grand Rapids area, to return in smaller numbers to Saginaw in October for the beet harvest. The rise of canneries and food-processing plants during the 1950s and 1960s continued to attract workers from depressed areas in Texas and Mexico; by 1957, seasonal agriculture in Michigan had climbed to a record 106,000 workers, including almost 15,000 braceros. Over half of the migrants in Michigan were employed in five counties—four in western Michigan and one along Saginaw Bay—primarily for fruits and vegetables.[46]

From the fields to the barrios, the church played a constructive role in easing the lives of Latinos, and even , on occasion, served as their advocate. The Grand Rapids and Saginaw dioceses developed special programs for the Mexican and Texan migrants. Since migrants were widely scattered and mobile, parish-based work was impracticable. The bishop of Saginaw, where Mexican workers were scattered on many farms, in 1947 organized a special diocesan work called the "Mexican Apostolate," administered by South Americans and Spaniards on leave from their dioceses or members of religious orders. Six missionary centers were established, each with a Spanish-speaking priest and one or two seminarians, who acted as local guides and visited migrant families scattered throughout the area, welcoming them and announcing Sunday Mass. Grassroots organizations and religious foundations offered migrant services to the tens of thousands of Mexicans and Mexican Americans in the state's seasonal labor force who made valuable economic contributions in the face of poor housing and inadequate educational facilities.[47]

A continuing concern of the midwestern Catholic hierarchy was the threat posed by Protestant missionaries in the region, which took on renewed force in the 1940s as the Home Missions Council oriented its activities toward migrants more aggressively, while soft-pedaling urban ministry. Its successor, the National Council of Churches, initiated a Migrant Ministry in 1950, a program that turned toward evangelism later in the decade. Since the migrants often returned yearly to the same employers, usually Protestant farmers, local churches saw them as likely converts. They often distributed donated food and clothing to the migrants and provided transportation to bring them to their services. Texas Mexicans tended to group together, and *tejana* women increasingly came north to work with their migrant husbands, settling out in cities in the late 1950s. Baptist congregations, in particular, made inroads among the *tejanos*, sponsoring nursery schools for the young in order to proselytize their parents.[48]

The Grand Rapids, Lansing, and Saginaw dioceses developed serious interests in helping agricultural workers, including braceros. During the 1950s the Bishops' Committee for the Spanish-Speaking borrowed priests from Mexico, especially from the Diocese of Guadalajara, to care for the foreign nationals. Growers in Lansing prohibited the diocese from conducting migrant programs in their camps, forcing the outreach programs to adopt nonconfrontational approaches with the farmers and companies and to stress religious over social aims. Rev. James Hickey, director of the Saginaw Apostolate, noted in 1953 that, "it seems better for the Apostolate, and our Mexican missionaries, to work directly for souls."[49] The Mexican priests and seminarians had their meager salaries, weekly expenses, and transportation costs paid. They, in turn, with the cooperation of local clergy (who often served as interpreters for the *tejanos*, most of whom did not speak Spanish well), conducted religious censuses and offered masses and Spanish sermons wherever migrants settled. The dioceses also sponsored recreational events and in many cases provided free medical care. Since the *tejano* migrants brought their families with them, the mission centers also offered first communions, confirmations, and marriage validations.[50] Reverend Hickey observed that these Mexican priests were very useful, particularly for the Mexican nationals, who greeted them "with real warmth, much hand-kissing and with remembrance of home."[51] In 1967 former migrant worker Rubén Alfaro of Lansing was named head of the Midwestern Division of the Bishops' Committee. Alfaro became an advocate not only within the church, but also in the public arena.

The organizing of farm workers in the Midwest in the 1960s was largely overshadowed by the effectiveness in California of César Chávez, whose work in the National Farm Workers Association (NFWA) began in 1962. In 1966 the NFWA affiliated with the AFL-CIO and became the United Farm Workers Organizing Committee (UFWOC). Organized labor in Michigan supported the ensuing California boycott

UFWOC march to Lansing by Michigan migrant workers and their supporters to present their grievances, March 1967 (F 3020-5M-7/69/ALHUA/UFOWC, Archives of Urban and Labor Affairs, Wayne State University).

and initially focused on winning a victory on the West Coast before moving out to other states. In the late 1960s, however, the UFW established its headquarters in Monroe County, over the opposition of farmers. César Chávez appointed Julian Herrera to direct the union's local organizing effort, and the Detroit Catholic Archdiocese covered the office and operating expenses.

During the heyday of the 1960s Chicano Movement, vocal support existed for Michigan farm workers, as highlighted by the seventy-mile "March for Migrants" from Saginaw to Lansing in 1967. Grape and lettuce boycott committees were established on several college campuses and in key cities such as Detroit. Later activities included inaugurating "secondary boycotts" of and picketing in front of supermarket chains carrying California table wine and grapes produced from nonunion labor, and engaging in fund-raising campaigns, such as that initiated for the November 1974 "Walk for Justice" from Kalamazoo to Grand Rapids. Throughout this period activists distributed leaflets and literature, often with the help of labor unions, and garnered the support of

Mexican Patriotic Committee marching in support of the farm workers in Lansing, 1967 (Archives of Urban and Labor Affairs, Wayne State University).

public officials and local clergy for the struggle that came to be known as *La Lucha*.[52]

Regional advisory committees organized letter-writing efforts to encourage active support of César Chávez and his fight for justice for farm workers, seeking solidarity with his well-publicized fasts. Other crops picked by unorganized migrants also came under scrutiny, and one 1972 UFW meeting in Phoenix offered a Statement of Concern, urging people nationwide to "refrain from eating or buying head [iceberg] lettuce unless it is clearly marked with the United Farm Workers Black Eagle Label." It was noted that union members picked only 15 percent of store lettuce, and personal commitments were requested of the local Catholic and public press and of parish priests. A national boycott was carried out against forty-five lettuce growers who signed agreements with the Teamsters' Union, amidst charges of manipulation and corruption, as it seemed that "probably a majority of field workers desired to be represented by the [UFW] and had no desire [for] the Teamsters."[53]

Despite solidarity with national efforts, midwestern Chicanos organized by unaffiliated, independent groups actually achieved the greatest successes in the region. Migrant workers in Wisconsin organized the region's first independent union, Obreros Unidos, in 1967, but it soon collapsed. The second effort, that of the Farm Labor Organizing Committee (FLOC), led by Báldemar Velásquez and others in northwestern Ohio, succeeded. Velásquez, born in Texas and raised in the Midwest, attempted to elevate the prospects of migrants in northwestern Ohio, near the Michigan border. At first the FLOC sought merely equal access to services, but soon it pursued unionization as an immediate priority, and in 1968 it organized tomato workers.[54]

A sharp decline in the size of the midwestern migrant force occurred from the mid-1960s to the early 1970s with the mechanization

Picketing in Detroit during the grape boycott, ca. 1968–70 (Archives of Urban and Labor Affairs, Wayne State University).

The UFW, La Lucha, and Michigan

The United Farm Workers Organizing Committee (UFWOC) worked to carry the farmworkers' struggle in Michigan across the United States (and as far even as Puerto Rico and Europe) to gain support for La Causa (The Cause), or La Lucha (The Struggle), a key aspect of the Chicano Movement. Organizers rented office facilities and made valuable contacts for the formation of boycott committees with outlets of the AFL-CIO while trying to gain the participation of independent unions. Beginning in the 1960s, they sought to inform the public about the problems of the farmworkers in the United States, forming task forces and distributing materials, including everything from buttons to bumper stickers. Letter-writing campaigns targeted the large supermarket chains, and issues eventually expanded from labor representation to the safety of workers and their families (primarily from the dangerous pesticides used). Cultural groups supporting the farm workers, such as California-based Luis Valdez and El Teatro Campesino, served both to inform and to entertain people in Michigan, especially Mexican Americans, as to the circumstances of their brethren in the Southwest.

César Chávez, along with UFW first vice-president Dolores Huerta and other union organizers, led a campaign to organize all agricultural workers within the UFW. A large concrete building near Delano, California, in the fertile San Joaquin Valley, served as its headquarters. The first target was the California grape industry. Chávez appealed to a wide array of groups and individual workers and began a national boycott that spread quickly. Farm workers were on strike against more than thirty California companies by 1968. In early 1970 the major grocery chains told the growers that they would buy only those California grapes labeled "UFWOC," and growers, in turn, required their workers to join the union. Chávez, a believer in the tactic of nonviolence adopted by Mahatma Gandhi and Martin Luther King Jr., later used boycotts to recruit melon and lettuce workers.

Michigan activists stood in solidarity with the Delano strikers and looked forward to their visits to open up new channels and garner public support. They petitioned prominent local individuals, as well as secular and religious organizations, to support what soon became a controversial national campaign. Many notable local and national leaders of the Roman Catholic Church spoke out against alleged instances of exploitation, greed, and injustice, urging people not to buy any grape products until California growers signed contracts with the UFW. Protestant groups, too, backed La Lucha in its opposition to nonunion growers of table grapes, head lettuce, and wine. These combined efforts sparked considerable opposition from agri-business, which spent large sums of money to discredit the efforts of farm workers. The UFW called upon the California state legislature and the U.S. Congress to enact legislation that would guarantee farm workers the right to organize and bargain collectively through a union of their choice. One campaign, coordinated with the National Farm Worker Ministry of the National Council of Churches, encouraged churches and synagogues to set aside 4–10 May 1975 as Farm Worker Week. During this week congregations were asked to remember the contributions of farm workers and to call attention to their struggle for social justice.

During the 1960s and 1970s numerous rallies and protests occurred among Michigan Chicanos in support of UFW boycotts and fund-raising. News of organizers having been arrested or physically accosted while attempting to talk with workers in the fields exacerbated existing tensions, as did battles over union elections for the country's hundreds of thousands of farm workers. The UFW, in its Second Constitutional Convention, held in Fresno, California, in August 1975, attracted over five hundred delegates representing farm workers and boycott offices nationally, including those in Michigan. The guest speakers included Leonard Woodcock, international president of the United Automobile Workers; the Canadian director and vice-president of the UAW; and representatives of the U.S. Catholic Conference and the Board of Homeland Ministries. Plans were made for future elections, boycotts, legislation, and other aspects of organizing. Resolutions passed calling for amnesty, citizenship, and the organizing of undocumented workers and for reaffirming the importance of nonviolence in supporting labor struggles around the world. Despite the successful passage of a law in California soon after that finally forcing the growers to hold union recognition elections, La Causa continued as a movement for workers' rights and civil rights. To some extent it paralleled earlier efforts of organized labor in industry and other sectors, but its uniquely Mexican-American leadership and identity gave it a distinctive tone that helped define a turbulent era.

of tasks previously performed by hand labor. Although FLOC originally was rural, it eventually shifted its concerns toward the urban circumstances of Mexican Americans. One result was the creation of the Migrant Community Development Corporation to develop gas co-ops and food co-ops. Velásquez often supported and marched with Chávez and other leaders when they visited Michigan. Sometimes the cause went well beyond the issue of agricultural labor, as was the case in Lansing's 1990 "Hispanic Unity March," an all-day affair that was punctuated by a riverfront Mass.

The national Mexican American organizations, the American G.I. Forum, and LULAC, meanwhile, opened offices in Michigan in the 1950s and began to encourage membership to provide a solid voice in social and political struggles. Other groups emerging from the civil rights movements of the 1970s and 1980s included the Mexican-American Legal Defense and Education Fund and the Puerto Rican Legal Defense and Educational Fund, which undertook efforts at reapportionment and redistricting in Detroit, where Latinos lacked numbers and clout. Efforts at political empowerment were generally much more successful in cities such as Chicago, where, today, the Latino proportion of the population, at 25 percent (as against 5 percent in Detroit), has given it the power of a "swing vote." The militant 1960s and early 1970s saw the rise of radical Mexican American and Puerto Rican organizations (the Brown Berets and the Young Lords, respectively). On the opposite end of the political spectrum stood the Cuban community, which did not seek Latino political alliances, largely because Cubans perceived themselves to be temporary political refugees anxiously awaiting an expeditious return to their country. The 1980s, however, saw the first significant electoral involvement of Cuban Americans nationally in the Cuban American National Foundation, based in Washington but with a strong power base in South Florida and in several key cities.[55]

Mexican American members of the Steelworkers Union at the Great Lakes Steel Corporation in Ecorse have played a prominent role in Detroit area civic life, supplying a core of trained and experienced community leaders. In the late 1960s these unionists, in the activist tradition of the Detroit working class, allied with prominent Catholic Church members to help establish Latin Americans United for Political

Action (LAUPA). This organization dedicated itself to furthering Latino participation in national, state, and local political campaigns. In 1969 a LAUPA proposal gained funding for the barrio's first federally supported social service agency targeting Latinos, La Sed (Latin Americans for Social and Economic Development). Subsequently, a plethora of urban community agencies arose, articulating Latino issues while providing services for Mexicans, Puerto Ricans, and other subgroups according to their varying needs.[56]

La Raza Unida, a coalition of Spanish-speaking organizations that began in El Paso in 1967, developed in Michigan, unlike its southwestern counterpart, as an organized pressure group rather than a political party. It criticized state governments for not having Spanish-speaking personnel, pressured the Catholic Church to teach Mexican American history and culture in its schools, and set up a scholarship fund for young migrant workers. Another important group, the Midwest Council of La Raza, formed in 1970 in South Bend, Indiana, with several members who had once been farm workers; it had its roots in the National Council of La Raza. The cumulative effect of internal differences among the Latinos, and even among the Mexican Americans, points to varying paths of assimilation. Older *tejanos* in Michigan and newcomers from Texas in the 1960s, for instance, developed antipathy toward one another, with the former seeing the latter as too radical and the latter, in turn, often assuming that the former were *vendidos* (sell-outs). Both sides, paradoxically, were equally voicing "American" sentiments, reflecting a generation gap evident among the general population as well.[57]

As the mechanization of agriculture increased in the 1970s, the flow of migrant farm labor from Texas and Mexico to Michigan declined markedly. Consequently, the number of rural migrants settling in Saginaw, Lansing, Flint, and Detroit diminished. In the cities, urban renewal and transportation programs disrupted existing community patterns during the 1950s and 1960s. Saginaw's federal projects, aimed at eliminating low-income housing, displaced part of that city's Mexican American population. Similarly, in Detroit a new highway bisecting the heart of Corktown separated a once-thriving commercial district from the newer areas of Latino settlement, helping to create the new nucleus to the southwest.

Changes in urban geography forced institutional adaptation in Lansing, as well, as the construction of an interstate highway in the 1960s forced the *colonia* to relocate in North Lansing. The existing Mexican church, Cristo Rey, was replaced by a community center catering to several ethnic groups, subordinating Mexican American customs to social programs. The Cristo Rey Social Center, however, attracted a wide range of Latino and other clergy and parishioners (including Cuban refugee priests and seminarians) and became the headquarters of the National Cursillo Movement, which reached out to a wide cross-section of the population, non-Mexicans and Mexicans alike. It anticipated some of the reforms and renewals of Vatican II that sought to further involve the laity in the life of the church, although it still restricted them to auxiliary roles. *Cursillistas,* who also gathered in Detroit-area parishes, in many ways ran counter to the traditionalism of the Mexican Catholic Church.[58]

Regional Migration and the Metropolis

According to the 2000 U.S. Census, since 1990 Latinos have accounted for more than half of the Midwest's net population growth. More than ever, globalism, suburbanization, and neighborhood change have emerged as crucial determinants of Latino migration across borders and regions. Mexicans account for over two-thirds of the Midwest's Latinos and for roughly three-quarters of Latino growth while the non-Latino white population has decreased. Other sending regions, however, such as Texas, the Caribbean, and the rest of Latin American, have included similar patterns of back and forth travel, the sending home of portions of industrial income, and the temporary placement of children with relatives abroad. Transnational institutions emerged in everything from employment to religion and extended kin networks have also expanded over increasingly wider geographic areas. Within the Midwest, Michigan ranks second only to Illinois in the number of Latino residents and in the number added since 1990 as the Mexican American population sustained a 60 percent increase statewide, to 221,000. The city of Detroit, meanwhile, once seen as the nation's premier example of urban decay, seemed at century's end to have halted its downward spiral of urban problems, although continued departure of white residents has halved their proportion in the city itself to merely 12 percent.[59]

Until the mid-1990s things did not look good for the city's economy, due to the clear cyclical downturn in the automobile industry, in
the making ever since the oil shocks of 1974. During the 1980s Detroit's
manufacturing base contracted as companies limited investments and
downsized the workforce and the United Automobile Workers (UAW)
struggled to preserve wage and benefits contracts that placed its members among the highest paid nationally. Many assembly lines closed,
including the main Cadillac plant at Clark and Michigan, and other
ancillary enterprises, such as the Fisher Body-Fleetwood factory, folded
operations. Both of these operations were located near the Southwest
Side barrio, and their loss caused many jobs to move outside the city.

Meanwhile, Detroit's automotive companies increased their production in Mexico, where a courtship had developed with the United
States in the 1960s with the building of low-wage assembly plants for
cars and other products, known as *maquiladoras,* just south of the border. Materials for the manufacture of all kinds of products were shipped
down in pieces and came back assembled. During the 1980s, Detroit
automakers continued to attempt to increase profit margins and
become more competitive with Japanese industry by moving even further south. By 1991 some 100,000 Mexicans worked for U.S. auto companies in scores of border plants with increasingly sophisticated
operations, while Mexico produced more than one million vehicles and
its exports surged 36 percent. The following year, General Motors closed
several U.S. plants in favor of those in Mexico, where workers earned
about one-eighth the salary of those in the Willow Run, Michigan, facil-
ity that was closed. Similarly, in the small town of Owosso, between the
Lansing and Flint industrial centers, many parts makers shut down,
costing hundreds of jobs, most of which were transplanted to Mexico.
New factories south of the border allowed the Big Three companies to
specialize in smaller cars designed for the Mexican market.[60]

Despite the seemingly inevitable decline of industry throughout
the Rust Belt, in the mid-1990s the return of general prosperity boosted
investment, employment levels, and property values. Detroit Mayor
Dennis Archer and business leaders committed billions of dollars to
rebuilding Chrysler Corporation and worked to expand and improve
several plants. New factories and industrial parks in the city's desig-

nated empowerment zone drastically lowered construction costs. In southwest Detroit, meanwhile, dozens of new businesses opened and even more expanded. Skilled immigrant labor rehabilitated run-down residences, and a surge of Mexican immigrants and some young artists moved in, upgrading entire blocks once ridden with gang violence and drug dealing. Local Roman Catholic parishes, for their part, added extra weekend Spanish Masses to accommodate the newest arrivals from Mexico, while parochial school registration increased.[61]

Within a few short years the barrio came to be hailed as a Mexican boomtown and a dynamic neighborhood, as the area's population nearly doubled (to over ninety thousand people), the total number of businesses rose markedly, and the real estate market jumped. *Taquerías,* Latin groceries, and other shops now line the Vernor-Junction commercial area, the barrio's hub. Residences are mostly single-family homes and two-flats built before 1920. Southwest Detroit offers a large supply of low-cost housing to white and Latino working-class residents; immigrants, in particular, have fueled business growth. International migration, meanwhile, has become further rooted in the social and economic structures of both Mexico and the United States. Immigration between sending areas and Latino communities increasingly has become organized through social networks forged from kinship ties and shared regional origins. Many of Southwest Detroit's forty thousand Mexican residents either came from Jalisco or have relatives there, a connection seen in the caravans of cars returning every January to attend fiestas honoring Jaliscan patron saints.[62]

Southwest Detroit, in the shadows of the Ambassador Bridge connecting with Windsor, Ontario, has, with the improved economy, become revitalized, both demographically and economically. Furthermore, despite being the city's most densely populated area it now has the second-lowest crime rate. This community, where Latinos, Poles, Appalachian whites, and Arab Americans live together (although Latinos are the only ethnic group that has the predominant part of its metropolitan population located in the Southwest), reaches to southeast Dearborn, near Ford's River Rouge plant. While they tend to live among whites, however, Latinos have avoided overwhelmingly African-American areas.[63]

The Detroit metropolitan area is the most segregated in the nation, a fact ameliorated only slightly by the influx of Latinos and Asian immigrants in the 1990s. Michigan's Latinos have been inclined to live among other ethnic groups, and they enjoy relatively high rates of intermarriage. Whereas in 1990 Latinos comprised less than 3 percent of the population in Detroit, the nation's tenth-largest city, in the 2000 census count their numbers stood at forty-seven thousand representing 5 percent of the total. Few newcomers are migrant workers; instead they come for permanent jobs in automobile factories and construction enterprises. Some leave when the weather gets cold and outdoor work slows, but the relatively high wages of $10.00 per hour in construction or landscaping serve as a magnet. To cut expenses, adult children often live with their parents as long as possible, pooling household wages.

The work of nonprofit groups has become especially important in refashioning the area. Several community agencies, notably the Southwest Detroit Business Association and the Mexicantown Commercial Development Corporation, supported by federal and local development grants, help channel growth, attract new businesses, and forestall blight. Their sponsorship of neighborhood fairs and other activities, moreover, has helped call attention to the need to preserve the urban core even as outer-ring communities expand. Colorful murals of Mexican images greet visitors to Bagley Street's Mexicantown strip—a few blocks filled with restaurants known for "authentic" ethnic cuisine. Elsewhere in southwest Detroit, however, one finds less glamorous areas, including underused train yards, trucking stations, and abandoned industrial sites.[64]

The Latino influx is not confined merely to the cities. Older residents and newcomers alike are also settling in suburbs, drawn by good schools and proximity to workplaces. Seventeen percent of Michigan's Latino population lives in Detroit's suburbs, led by Oakland County, where the Latino population has increased by almost half, to 25,000. While Detroit has dipped to its lowest population in eighty years, job-rich Oakland County has added 111,000 residents since 1990, a 10 percent boost, including many Latinos (whose numbers in parts of the central county exceed 20 percent of the population). Other significant concentrations exist in Macomb County, where the Latino population

Pablo Davis, the artist of this mural in Southwest Detroit depicting the down-town skyline, the Ambassador Bridge, and southwest Detroit (background), left Mexico at age sixteen to see Diego Rivera paint at the Detroit Institute of the Arts. The original mural was restored by the City of Detroit in the summer of 1997 (Southwest Detroit Development Corporation).

jumped 56 percent in the 1990s, to 12,000. Latinos have also settled in large numbers recently in Pontiac. Many upwardly mobile Mexican Americans, Puerto Ricans, and Cubans have joined non-Latinos in the northern suburbs of Warren and Livonia, as well as in neighboring Downriver communities such as River Rouge, Ecorse, and Allen Park, challenging the historic image of Detroit suburbs as exclusively white preserves.[65]

Western Michigan's Hispanic population has traditionally been concentrated in the more rural areas. In the 1990s, however, Latinos moved into urban and suburban areas, driven mainly by an influx of Mexican immigrants. In the greater Grand Rapids area, Latinos in 2000 comprised over 6 percent of the population (69,000 persons), a more than threefold increase since 1990; the Mexican population alone jumped 185 percent, from 6,000 to 17,000. Grand Rapids, Michigan's second-largest city, had its population grow by 26,000 during the 1990s, largely due to the huge influx of Latino residents, more than offsetting a decline in the white population. By comparison, the population of Lansing, with fewer Latinos arriving, dropped 6 percent over the same period. One significant trend, indicative of an ongoing "brain drain" of university-educated persons seeking opportunities in the upper Midwest, is the new wave of Puerto Rican professionals who have begun migrating directly from the island to work for pharmaceutical companies in Kalamazoo and environs.[66]

Contemporary Ethnicity and Leadership

The Latino presence in Michigan increasingly involves integration into all areas of the state and integration into a wide variety of the state's political, social, and cultural institutions. Michigan's Mexican American communities, concentrated since the mid-1900s around Detroit, the "thumb," and a few counties bordering Lake Michigan, now extend throughout the Lower Peninsula and even show some inroads in parts of the Upper Peninsula. Areas of largely Puerto Rican ancestry are similar, but more tightly bound to the cities. Cubans are dispersed more generally throughout entire metropolitan areas. The predominantly middle-class Cubans, Colombians, Argentinians, and others have tended to live outside of the barrio, sharing few socioeconomic characteristics with barrio residents. Among all Latino groups, the second generation has increasingly participated within both major political parties. Wherever they settle, Latinos defy facile racial and ethnic classification.[67]

The Catholic Church has historically organized diverse Latino groups while acknowledging their distinctive cultures, and, often pushed from within by its parishioners, it has helped spur important contributions. The Day of the Dead (*Día de los Muertos*) is a Mexican religious celebration held in memory of the deceased that combines

Catholic ritual with pre-Columbian beliefs about life and death. In many homes a ritual altar is prepared to honor the returned dead souls on 1 and 2 November, and this is often combined with the Catholic Mass for the dead held in the local church. The more Americanized Mexicans observe the celebration of Halloween over the Day of the Dead.

In December, the reenactment of the journey of Mary and Joseph, *Las Posadas,* is still celebrated in many parishes. The Virgin Mary is placed on a donkey with St. Joseph at the side on a platform. The pilgrims are taken from house to house and the rosary is prayed. Wherever Catholics of Mexican ancestry are found, the Virgin of Guadalupe evokes feelings of love, protection, faith, and hope, and in many mixed Latino communities Guadalupe celebrations reach out to Puerto Ricans and Central and South Americans as well. One second-generation Mexican American noted that "everyone is involved and there is a sense of unity. [We are not] just celebrating the feast of the Patroness of Mexico, but the patroness of all the Americas."[68]

The church has only recently begun fully to address the broad spectrum of issues that affect contemporary Latino communities. Many of these concerns are of a secular nature, such as housing, unemployment, and the need to raise the level of educational aspirations and performance. Others deal with technology, migration, and the need to send remittances to family members south of the border. Indeed, Latino socioeconomic indicators are among the lowest in Michigan. Although many Mexican Americans, Puerto Ricans, and Cubans enjoy the stability of middle-class life, many plan to return home. Unlike European immigrants, who frequently broke ties with the mother country, pioneer Latino migrants usually are fairly close—geographically and culturally—to their ancestral roots, a fact that the church and other institutions have come to understand.

More Latino Catholics in Detroit are reaching out to other religions, while the church tries to figure out how to reach out to them. Although disenchantment has also been growing among non-Latinos, the Latino flight appears more alarming because of the historic loyalty of that group and the fact that they number over one-third of U.S. Catholics. Whereas Latinos in earlier eras belonged to mainstream Protestant denominations, an estimated 20 percent have joined

Pentecostal and other evangelical congregations, which are usually led by Latino pastors. These churches in southeast Michigan often pool their resources and personnel. In response to the religious competition, as well as in an attempt to better to serve their members, Catholic parishes with Spanish or bilingual Masses are now found in communities throughout Michigan.[69]

Latinos of all backgrounds regain a sense of identity through participation in cultural events such as Detroit's annual "Unity in the Community" festival in Clark Park and the June Mexicantown Fiesta, featuring homeland remembrances in food and entertainment, artists' exhibitions, and even the occasional Mexican rodeo. Other such events include Pontiac's annual "Puerto Rican Festival," featuring both Salsa and Tex-Mex bands; and a separate Mexican Festival sponsored by the city's Mexican Mutualista Club. Saginaw holds a Ballet Cultural Azteca that highlights *mariachi* music, and every September Grand Rapids hosts its Mexican Festival, one of Michigan's longest-running ethnic events. The Downriver Latin American Club sponsors a Mexican-American Festival over Memorial Day. In the realm of business, too, Latino organizations have been established throughout the state, including the Michigan Hispanic Chamber of Commerce, the Hispanic Business Alliance, and the Detroit Hispanic Chamber of Commerce. Many of the state's universities, meanwhile, offer venues for learning Spanish and for exploring Latin American culture and, increasingly, the hybrid cultures and histories of Latino communities in the United States.[70]

Michigan's growing Latino community has attracted much attention from political candidates. Around the state, a handful of Latinos hold elected office and political appointments in cities such as Detroit, Pontiac, and Lansing; similarly, Grand Rapids has sporadically elected Latinos to public offices. A Puerto Rican recently became the first Latino elected to the Washtenaw County Board of Commissioners. In addition, for the first time in Michigan's history, two Latinos are now serving in the state legislature. State Senator Báldemar García is a Republican whose district covers Clinton, Shiawassee, and Livingston counties. State Representative Belda Garza, a Democrat representing a district that encompasses southwest Detroit and River Rouge, reflects the increasing participation of Latina women—long active in the

Latino Music and Culture

Cuban music was derived from a fusion of Spanish and African elements. Afro-Cuban musical forms directly influencing salsa musicians include the son, the rumba, and the religious music of the bata used in Santería. The conga, which takes its name from a large African drum, had its origin in these festivities. African ceremonies require the appropriate music, and drums summon the spirits in ceremonials adopting special rhythms interwoven with all aspects of life. In its transplanted form, Cuban practitioners of Santería have helped perpetuate the rhythms. Musical transculturation, a process of cultural blending, occurred in Cuba and elsewhere in Latin America where residents influenced each other across ethnic, racial, and class lines.

Puerto Rico also has influential and distinctive musical styles. In its broad outlines, Puerto Rican music is fairly similar to that of Cuba, although it has fewer African-derived characteristics, except in modes like the bomba, which uses two or three drums in the West African style; voices open unaccompanied in this form, and then the drums enter dramatically. The plena, also uniquely Puerto Rican, has a stronger Spanish influence. The merengue, the national music of the Dominican Republic, first became popular in Santo Domingo around 1850 and, like many popular styles in the Caribbean, it is dance music. It has had international influence, and it, too, is exemplified by the use of the bongos and conga drums.

Large Latino communities in New York—and later in other U.S. cities, including Miami, Los Angeles, and Detroit—provided portals for innovations from Cuba,

workplace—in public and professional life. There is no citywide Latino representation in Detroit, largely because of an at-large system for council elections that dilutes Latino voting strength. In the face of numerous challenges, however, Latinos continue to seek self-propelled mechanisms for political empowerment.[71]

Clearly, a thorough understanding of the various manifestations of Latino diversity offers a window on larger social questions in the United States and elsewhere in the Americas. Socioeconomic and other factors account for significant underrepresentation among Michigan Latinos, while the questions of how, and with whom, to form alliances, and

Puerto Rico, and other locations in the Western Hemisphere. The son, based on a combination of guitars and percussion instruments, constituted an important element of what during the 1960s evolved as salsa music in the mainland United States. It began in Oriente Province and by 1916 had made its way to Havana. As a steady influx of large numbers of Cubans and Puerto Ricans came to the United States, by the 1930s there arose a large market for Spanish-Caribbean music. A fusion occurred between Caribbean music and U.S. jazz, rhythm and blues, and to a lesser extent, rock and roll. The forces of migration, international marketing, and cultural change have sparked numerous innovations in what has come to be known as salsa, a composite of the aforementioned influences.

Tex-Mex, or conjunto, music, arrived in Michigan with the tejano migration in the early decades of the twentieth century. One of the brightest stars of this early era of Mexican-American music was Lydia Mendoza, whose first recordings were made in 1928 with her family in Texas. The group included the songs of the day, "El Rancho Grande" and other tunes popular on both sides of the border among Mexicans and tejanos. After their early recordings they traveled north to Michigan in the 1930s, when Lydia was still a child, entertaining in cities and towns along the migrant stream. After a two-year stint in Detroit, the family returned to San Antonio and Lydia launched a solo career lasting for many years.

The music of Michigan Latinos survives in the cultures of individual families, in festivals, and in special events as well as in bilingual radio broadcasts.

indeed any broad leadership strategy, point to amorphous and widely diffused leadership. One fundamental barrier preventing further marshaling of resources and energy among Mexicans, Mexican Americans, Puerto Ricans, Cubans, and others is the lack of a unified cultural identity transcending nationalism. Even in the southwest Detroit Latino melting pot, ethnic consciousness often results in encapsulation rather than solidarity, although a strong working-class background binds all groups. The degree to which this cultural, economic, and political expression matures will largely determine future Latino contributions; in many respects the greatest successes are yet to come.

Notes

1. The term *Latino* is used here—although *Hispanic* is synonymous—for people of Latin American origin living permanently or semipermanently within the boundaries of the United States.
2. Francisco A. Rosales, "Mexican Immigration to the Urban Midwest during the 1920s" (Ph.D. diss., Indiana University, 1978), 92, 99, 107.
3. Dennis N. Valdes, "Betabeleros: The Formation of an Agricultural Proletariat in the Midwest, 1897–1930," *Labor History* 30 (fall 1989): 556–58, 562.
4. Eduard A. Skendzel, *Detroit's Pioneer Mexicans: A Study of the Mexican Colony in Detroit* (Grand Rapids, Mich.: Littleshield Press, 1980), 7, 27–30.
5. Zaragosa Vargas, *Proletarians of the North: A History of Mexican Industrial Workers in Detroit and the Midwest, 1917–1933* (Berkeley: University of California Press, 1993), 20.
6. Zaragosa Vargas, "Life and Community in the 'Wonderful City of the Magic Motor': Mexican Immigrants in 1920s Detroit," *Michigan Historical Review* 15 (spring 1989): 49; John R. Weeks and Joseph Spielberg Benitez, "The Cultural Demography of Midwestern Chicano Communities," in *The Chicano Experience*, Stanley A. West and June Macklin, eds. (Boulder, Colo.: Westview Press, 1979), 231.
7. Louis C. Murillo, "The Detroit Michigan 'Colonia' from 1920 to 1932:

Implications for Social and Educational Policy" (Ph.D. diss., Michigan State University, 1981), 33, 34.

8. Norman D. Humphrey, "Employment Patterns of Mexicans in Detroit," *Monthly Labor Review* 61 (November 1945): 914, 921.

9. Norman D. Humphrey, "Mexican Repatriation from Michigan: Public Assistance in Historical Perspective," *Social Service Review* 15 (September 1941): 501–3, 512; Vargas, "Life and Community," 65, 67. For an account of repatriates in Mexico, see Paul S. Taylor, *A Spanish-Mexican Peasant Community: Arandas in Jalisco, Mexico* (Berkeley: University of California Press, 1933).

10. Rosales, "Mexican Immigration," 107–10.

11. Kay D. Willson, "The Historical Development of Migrant Labor in Michigan Agriculture" (Master's thesis, Michigan State University, 1978), 22–25, 39–43; Carey McWilliams, "Mexicans to Michigan," in *A Documentary History of the Mexican Americans,* ed. Wayne Moquin (1941; reprint, New York: Praeger, 1971), 311–14. See also Carey McWilliams, *Ill Fares the Land: Migrants and Migratory Labor in the United States* (Boston: Little Brown and Company, 1942).

12. Valdes, "Betabeleros," 59–61.

13. Reymundo Cardenas, "The Mexican in Adrian," *Michigan History* 42 (September 1958): 346–49.

14. Quoted in Melvin G. Holli, "The Founding of Detroit by Cadillac," *Michigan Historical Review* 27 (spring 2001): 135.

15. "The Redemptorists in Detroit," *Holy Redeemer Weekly* 26 (22 July 1951): 1, 3, 4; Brian Wilson, "The Spirit of the Motor City: Three Hundred Years of Religious History in Detroit," *Michigan Historical Review* 27 (spring 2001): 25.

16. Skendzel, *Detroit's Pioneer Mexicans,* 29; Ralph Janis, "The Brave New World that Failed: Patterns of Parish Social Structure in Detroit, 1880–1940" (Ph.D. diss., University of Michigan, 1972), 169.

17. Father Gabriel Ginard to Monsignor Doyle, 5 March 1926, Our Lady of Guadalupe file, Archives of the Archdiocese of Detroit (hereafter *OLG*).

18. "Jacobus" to Monsignor Doyle, 14 September 1927, *OLG.*

19. Father Peter T. Fiexa, speech at St. Anne's Church, 18 September 1939, cited in Norman D. Humphrey, "The Mexican Peasant in Detroit" (Ph.D. diss., University of Michigan, 1943), 157.

20. Simón Muñoz et al., Detroit, to Most Illustrious and Reverend Lord Bishop of the Catholic Diocese of Detroit, Michigan, 18 October 1932, *OLG*.

21. Petition of the Altar Society to Bishop Gallagher, 14 May 1936, *OLG*; telegram from Mexican Committee to Bishop Gallagher, 13 July 1927, *OLG*.

22. Josefina González, quoted in Margarita Valdez, ed., *Tradiciones del Pueblo: Traditions of Three Mexican Feast Days in Southwest Detroit* (Detroit: Casa de Unidad Cultural Arts and Media Center, 1990), 19; see also Skendzel, *Detroit's Pioneer Mexicans*, 35, 36.

23. For background on Father Kern, see Genevieve M. Casey, *Father Clem Kern: Conscience of Detroit* (Detroit: Marygrove College, 1989).

24. Valdez, *Tradiciones del Pueblo*, 13.

25. This "labor migration" occurred as the island economy underwent modernization under a program of economic development that offered tax incentives for investment in capital-intensive manufacturing enterprises by U.S. companies.

26. Edwin Maldonado, "Contract Labor and the Origin of Puerto Rican Communities in the United States," in *Forging a Community: The Latino Experience in Northwest Indiana, 1919–1975*, ed. James B. Lane and Edward J. Escobar (Chicago: Cattails Press, 1987), 201, 203–4.

27. "Beet Airlift," *Detroit Tribune*, 14 June 1950, 1.

28. For background on the evolution of Puerto Rican settlement on the U.S. mainland see Joseph P. Fitzpatrick, *Puerto Rican Americans: The Meaning of Migration to the Mainland* (New York: Prentice-Hall, 1987).

29. Father Clement Kern, Holy Trinity Church, Detroit, to William F. Kelly, director, Social Action Department, Diocese of Brooklyn, 23 November 1952, folder 3B, Redemptorist Archives, Brooklyn, New York.

30. For background on the Cuban exodus and the Cuban-American experience, see Thomas D. Boswell and James R. Curtis, *The Cuban-American Experience: Culture, Images, and Perspectives* (Totowa, N.J.: Rowman and Allanheld, 1983) and Felix Masud-Piloto, *From Welcomed Exiles to Illegal Immigrants: Cuban Migration to the U.S., 1959–1995* (Lanham, Md.: Rowman and Littlefield, 1996).

31. John F. Thomas, director, Cuban Refugee Program, Department of Health, Education, and Welfare, in United States Senate, Committee on the Judiciary, *Resettlement of Cuban Refugees* (Washington, D.C.: Government Printing Office, 1964), 186. Protestantism, certainly not unknown during

the years of the Cuban Republic, had gained a strong foothold in the country by the beginning of the revolution. In fact, several Protestants took leadership roles in the early years of Castro's rule, before becoming disillusioned with the anti-religious persecution of the early 1960s.

32. Church World Service, "Cuban Refugee Flights" (1 November 1963), in United States Senate, *Resettlement of Cuban Refugees*, 23, 30.

33. Quoted in United States Senate, Committee on the Judiciary, *Cuban Refugee Problem: Hearings before the Subcommittee to Investigate Problems Connected with Refugees and Escapees*, part 2, Grand Rapids, Michigan, 14 October 1963 (Washington, D.C.: Government Printing Office, 1963), 186.

34. United States Senate, *Cuban Refugee Problem*, 187.

35. José Tagle, quoted in United States Senate, *Cuban Refugee Problem*, 225.

36. United States Senate, *Cuban Refugee Problem*, 241, 244.

37. Stanley J. Davis, quoted in United States Senate, *Cuban Refugee Problem*, 206.

38. United States Senate, *Cuban Refugee Problem*, 195, 236.

39. Carol Berry, *A Survey of the Holland Spanish-Speaking Community* (East Lansing: Michigan State University Institute for Community Developemtn, 1970), 1, 17, 40. See also Anne M. Santiago, *Life in the Industrial Heartland: A Profile of Latinos in the Midwest*, Institute Report no. 2 (East Lansing: Julian Samora Research Institute, 1990).

40. *Resettlement Recap: A Periodic Report from the Cuban Refugee Center* (Washington, D.C.: U.S. Department of Health, Education, and Welfare, 1967), 3.

41. For coverage of Cuban and Cuban-American entrepreneurs in Miami, see Alejandro Portes and Robert L. Bach, *Latin Journey: Cuban and Mexican Immigrants in the United States* (Berkeley: University of California Press, 1985).

42. David A. Badillo, "Latino/Hispanic History since 1965: The Collective Transformation of Regional Minorities," in *Hispanic Catholic Culture in the U.S.: Issues and Concerns*, ed. Jay P. Dolan and Allan Figueroa Deck (South Bend, Ind.: University of Notre Dame Press, 1994), 65.

43. Fanny Tabares, "Reflections on South American Catholics in the United States, 1997," in *Presente! U.S. Latino Catholics from Colonial Origins to the Present*, ed. Timothy Matovina and Gerald E. Poyo (Maryknoll, N.Y.: Orbis Books, 2000), 134.

44. Tabares, "Reflections on South American Catholics," 135–37.

45. Farm Placement Service, Texas State Employment Service, "Supplement to Origins and Problems of Texas Migratory Farm Labor" (Austin: Texas Employment Compensation Commission, 1941), 3, 9, 12; Cardenas, "The Mexican in Adrian," 346.

46. James A. Forester, "Migratory Children in the Edgewood School District, 1950–1951 (Master's thesis, Trinity University, 1952), 14; Cardenas, "The Mexican in Adrian," 350.

47. James A. Hickey, director, Mexican Apostolate, Saginaw, Michigan, to Archbishop Robert E. Lucey, San Antonio, 15 October 1952, reel 85, Robert E. Lucey Papers, University of Notre Dame Archives (hereafter UNDA).

48. Ibid.; Sister Mary E. Thomas, "A Study of the Causes and Consequences of the Economic Status of Migratory Farm Workers in Illinois, Indiana, Michigan, and Wisconsin, 1940–1958 (Ph.D. diss., University of Notre Dame, 1960), 267–68.

49. Rev. James A. Hickey, director, Mexican Apostolate, Diocese of Saginaw, to Archbishop Robert E. Lucey, San Antonio, 8 July 1953, Reel 16, Lucey Papers, UNDA.

50. Hickey to Lucey, 8 July 1953.

51. Robert E. Lucey, "Analysis of Report by Father Radtke Concerning Migrant Mexican Workers in the North Central States," 15 October 1952, 1, 2, Robert E. Lucey Papers, UNDA. See also Rev. Joseph H. Crosthwait, field representative, Bishops' Committee for the Spanish Speaking, San Antonio, "Excerpts from Report of Field Trip to the Northern States," October 1957, 5, UNDA.

52. Richard Santillan, "Latino Politics in the Midwestern United States: 1915–1986," in *Latinos and the Political System*, ed. F. Chris Garcia (South Bend, Ind.: University of Notre Dame Press, 1988), 100; Rodolfo Acuna, *Occupied America: A History of Chicanos* (New York: Harper and Row, 1981), 278–79. On the Michigan boycotts, see United Farm Workers State and Local Boycotts, Administration file, in the César Chávez Collection, Walter P. Reuther Library, Wayne State University.

53. Rubén R. Alfaro, executive director, Midwestern Regional Office, Division for the Spanish-Speaking, U.S. Catholic Conference, Lansing, Michigan, to Most Rev. Leo A. Pursley, Diocese of Fort Wayne-South Bend, 19 June 1972, Fort Wayne Diocese Archives.

54. For background, see John A. Soto, "Mexican American Community Leadership for Education" (Ph.D. diss., University of Michigan, 1974) and Dennis N. Valdes, *Al Norte: Agricultural Workers in the Great Lakes Region, 1917–1970* (Austin: University of Texas Press, 1991).

55. Santillan, "Latino Politics," 109, 110, 112.

56. Gumersindo Salas and Isabel Salas, "The Mexican Community of Detroit," in *Immigrants and Migrants: The Detroit Ethnic Experience*, ed. David W. Hartman (Detroit: New University Thought Publishing Company, 1974), 381, 382; Steve Babson, "Living in Two Worlds: The Immigrant Experience in Detroit," *Michigan Quarterly Review* 25 (spring 1986): 377–80.

57. Willson, "Historical Development of Migrant Labor," 46, 49, 53–54.

58. Harvey M. Choldin and Grafton D. Trout, *Mexican Americans in Transition: Migration and Employment in Michigan Cities* (East Lansing: Michigan State University Agricultural Experiment Station, 1969), 356, 374, 381; Julie Burns, *Viva Cristo Rey* (Lansing, Mich.: M-R Publications, 1980), 7, 174; Marietta L. Baba and Malvina H. Abonyii, *Mexicans of Detroit* (Detroit: Wayne State University Press, 1979), 65, 66, 70. See also Refugio I. Rochin, Anne M. Santiago, and Karla S. Dickey, *Migrant and Seasonal Workers in Michigan's Agriculture: A Study of Their Contributions, Characteristics, Needs, and Services*, Institute Research Report no. 1 (East Lansing: Julian Samora Research Institute, Michigan State University, 1989).

59. *Nexo* [Newsletter of the Julian Samora Research Institute] 2 (winter 1994): 1.

60. Kevin Boyle, "The Ruins of Detroit: Exploring the Urban Crisis in the Motor City," *Michigan Historical Review* 27 (spring 2001): 111, 123; Bernard Ortiz de Montellano and Isabel Salas, "Spanish Origin Population in Detroit," Census Discussion Papers, Center for Urban Studies, Wayne State University, no. 4 (July 1984), 1; "Detroit South," *Business Week* (16 March 1992): 98, 101–3.

61. Unless otherwise indicated, newspaper articles hereafter have omitted pagination, as their web versions were consulted through Internet archives of the various local newspapers. "Firms Snap Up Sites: Manufacturers Find Detroit Desirable," *Detroit Free Press*, 17 April 1997; "Detroit Neighborhood Group Grooms Area for New Business," *Detroit Free Press*, 14 October 1998. On earlier conditions see, for example, "Youth Gangs Threaten SW Detroit," *Michigan Catholic* 119 (March 1991): 1, 2.

62. "Immigrants Help Fuel City's Boom: Newcomers Keep Up Diversity Tradition," *Detroit Free Press*, 30 March 2001; "Mexican Immigrants Lead a Revival," *New York Times*, 18 December 1999.

63. "Southwest Detroit Buys into the Boom" *Detroit Free Press*, 13 June 1999; "Southwest Detroit: Neighborhood Remains the City's Most Diverse," *Detroit News and Free Press*, 1 April 2001.

64. "Detroit under 1 Million: Suburbs Keep Booming," *Detroit Free Press*, 29 March 2001; "High Hopes for Future: Macomb, Oakland Counties Lead Way in Mexican Growth," *Detroit Free Press*, 29 March 2001.

65. "Population Change and Ethnicity in Southeastern Michigan, 1980–2000," *Detroit Free Press*, 29 March 2001; "Detroit under 1 Million: Suburbs Keep Booming," *Detroit Free Press*, 29 March 2001.

66. "Grand Rapids 9th in Hispanics' Places to Live: Michigan Sees Growth in Community in '90s," *Detroit Free Press*, 16 September 1999); "Hispanics Drive Grand Rapids' Surge," *Detroit Free Press*, 31 March 31, 2001. See also Valerie Menard, "Top Ten Cities for Hispanics," *Hispanic Magazine* (July–August 1999).

67. "Economic Downsizing Causes Cities to Lose Residents," *Detroit Free Press*, 29 March 2001.

68. Father Juan José González, quoted in Valdez, *Tradiciones del Pueblo*, 28. See also "Copy of Catholic Icon on Display: Our Lady of Guadalupe Likeness Touring State," *Detroit Free Press*, 20 March 2001.

69. "Following a Voice, He Breaks away from His Faith," *Detroit News*, 23 December 1990, 6A, "Hispanic Catholics: Losing Faith," *Detroit News*, 23 December 1990, 1A, 6A; "Church Puts out Welcome Mat: Catholic Bishops Try to Spread Faith to Immigrants," *Detroit Free Press*, 15 November 2000.

70. Kevin Lane, "Stories Behind the Names: Clark (Park)/Hubbard/Richard," *El Barrio* [Detroit] 1 (spring/summer 1991): 29.

71. "More Hispanics Hold Office, but Barriers Hold up More Progress," *Detroit Free Press*, 1 October 1998; "Hispanic Senator Takes Pride in Success: Michigan Lawmaker Recruiting for GOP," *Detroit Free Press*, 2 April 2001; "Hispanic Population, Influence Rise: State Shows 61 Percent Gain," *Ann Arbor News*, 1 April 2001, A1.

For Further Reference

Books and Articles

Acuna, Rodolfo. *Occupied America: A History of Chicanos*. New York: Harper and Row, 1981.

Baba, Marietta L., and Malvina H. Abonyii. *Mexicans of Detroit*. Detroit: Wayne State University Press, 1979.

Babson, Steve. "Living in Two Worlds: The Immigrant Experience in Detroit." *Michigan Quarterly Review* 25 (spring 1986): 369–85.

Badillo, David A. "The Catholic Church and the Making of Mexican-American Parish Communities in the Midwest." In *Mexican Americans and the Catholic Church, 1900–1965*. Edited by Jay P. Dolan and Gilberto M. Hinojosa, 237–308. South Bend, Ind.: University of Notre Dame Press, 1994.

———. "Latino/Hispanic History since 1965: The Collective Transformation of Regional Minorities." In *Hispanic Catholic Culture in the U.S.: Issues and Concerns*. Edited by Jay P. Dolan and Allan Figueroa Deck, 50–76. South Bend, Ind.: University of Notre Dame Press, 1994.

Berry, Carol. "A Survey of the Holland Spanish-Speaking Community." East Lansing: Michigan State University Institute for Community Development, 1970.

Boswell, Thomas D., and James R. Curtis. *The Cuban-American Experience: Culture, Images, and Perspectives*. Totowa, N.J.: Rowman and Allanheld, 1983.
69

Boyle, Kevin. "The Ruins of Detroit: Exploring the Urban Crisis in the Motor City." *Michigan Historical Review* 27 (spring 2001): 109–27.

Burns, Julie. *Viva Cristo Rey.* Lansing: M-R Publications, 1980.

Cardenas, Reymundo. "The Mexican in Adrian." *Michigan History* 42 (September 1958): 343–52.

Casey, Genevieve M. *Father Clem Kern: Conscience of Detroit.* Detroit: Marygrove College, 1989.

Center for Puerto Rican Studies. *Labor Migration under Capitalism: The Puerto Rican Experience.* New York: Monthly Review Press, 1979.

Choldin, Harvey M., and Grafton D. Trout. *Mexican Americans in Transition: Migration and Employment in Michigan Cities.* East Lansing: Michigan State University Agricultural Experiment Station, 1969.

De Montellano, Bernard Ortiz, and Isabel Salas. "Spanish Origin Population in Detroit." Census Discussion Papers: Metro Detroit in the '80's, no. 4. Detroit: MIMIC/CUS Wayne State University, 1984.

Farm Placement Service, Texas State Employment Service. "Supplement to Origins and Problems of Texas Migratory Farm Labor." Austin: Texas Employment Compensation Commission, November 1941.

Fitzpatrick, Joseph P. *Puerto Rican Americans: The Meaning of Migration to the Mainland.* New York: Prentice-Hall, 1987.

Forester, James A. "Migratory Children in the Edgewood School District, 1950–1951." Master's thesis, Trinity University, 1952.

Gleason, James. *Apostolic Blessing: On the Occasion of the 100th Anniversary of Holy Redeemer Parish, 1880–1980.* Detroit: Holy Redeemer, 1980.

Holli, Melvin G. "The Founding of Detroit by Cadillac." *Michigan Historical Review* 27 (spring 2001): 129–36.

Humphrey, Norman D. "Mexican Repatriation from Michigan: Public Assistance in Historical Perspective." *Social Service Review* 15 (September 1941): 497–513.

———. "The Mexican Peasant in Detroit." Ph.D. diss., University of Michigan, 1943.

———. "Employment Patterns of Mexicans in Detroit." *Monthly Labor Review* 61 (November 1945): 913–23.

Janis, Ralph. "The Brave New World that Failed: Patterns of Parish Social Structure in Detroit, 1880–1940." Ph.D. diss., University of Michigan, 1972.

Lane, Kevin. "Stories Behind the Names: Clark (Park)/ Hubbard/ Richard." *EL*

Barrio [Detroit] 1 (spring/summer 1991): 29–31.

Maldonado, Edwin. "Contract Labor and the Origin of Puerto Rican Communities in the United States." In *Forging a Community: The Latino Experience in Northwest Indiana, 1919–1975*. Edited by James B. Lane and Edward J. Escobar, 201–12. Chicago: Cattails Press, 1987.

Masud-Piloto, Felix. *From Welcomed Exiles to Illegal Immigrants: Cuban Migration to the U.S., 1959–1995*. Lanham, Md.: Rowman & Littlefield, 1996.

McWilliams, Carey. "Mexicans to Michigan." *Common Ground* (Autumn 1941). In *A Documentary History of the Mexican Americans*. Edited by Wayne Moquin, 310–14. New York: Praeger, 1971.

———. *Ill Fares the Land: Migrants and Migratory Labor in the United States*. Boston: Little Brown and Company, 1942.

Murillo, Louis C. "The Detroit Michigan 'Colonia' from 1920 to 1932: Implications for Social and Educational Policy." Ph.D. diss., Michigan State University, 1981.

Ortiz de Montellano, Bernard, and Isabel Salas. "Spanish Origin Population in Detroit." Census Discussion Papers, Center for Urban Studies, Wayne State University, no. 4, July 1984.

Portes, Alejandro, and Robert L. Bach. *Latin Journey: Cuban and Mexican Immigrants in the United States*. Berkeley: University of California Press, 1985.

Resettlement Recap: A Periodic Report from the Cuban Refugee Center. Washington, D.C.: U.S. Department of Health, Education, and Welfare, 1967.

Rochin, Refugio I., Anne M. Santiago, and Karla S. Dickey. *Migrant and Seasonal Workers in Michigan's Agriculture: A Study of Their Contributions, Characteristics, Needs, and Services*. Institute Research Report no. 1. East Lansing: Julian Samora Research Institute, Michigan State University, November 1989.

Rosales, Francisco A. "Mexican Immigration to the Urban Midwest during the 1920s." Ph.D. Diss., Indiana University, 1978.

Salas, Gumersindo, and Isabel Salas. "The Mexican Community of Detroit." In *Immigrants and Migrants: The Detroit Ethnic Experience*. Edited by David W. Hartman, 374–87. Detroit: New University Thought Publishing Company, 1974.

Santiago, Anne M. "Life in the Industrial Heartland: A Profile of Latinos in the

Midwest." Institute Research Report no. 2. East Lansing: Julian Samora
Research Institute, May 1990.

Santillan, Richard. "Latino Politics in the Midwestern United States: 1915–1986."
In *Latinos and the Political System*. Edited by F. Chris Garcia, 99–118. South
Bend, Ind.: University of Notre Dame Press, 1988.

Skendzel, Eduard A. *Detroit's Pioneer Mexicans: A Study of the Mexican Colony in
Detroit*. Grand Rapids, Mich.: Littleshield Press, 1980.

Sommers, Laurie Kay. "Inventing Latinismo: The Creation of 'Hispanic'
Panethnicity in the United States." *Journal of American Folklore* 104 (winter 1991): 32–53.

Soto, John A. "Mexican American Community Leadership for Education." Ph.D.
diss., University of Michigan, 1974.

Tabares, Fannie. "Reflections of South American Catholics in The United States,
1997," In *Presente! U.S Latino Catholics from Colonial Origins to the Present*.
Edited by Timothy Matovina and Gerald E. Poyo. Maryknoll, N.Y.: Orbis
Books, 2000.

Taylor, Paul S. *A Spanish-Mexican Peasant Community: Arandas in Jalisco,
Mexico*. Berkeley: University of California Press, 1933.

Thomas, Mary E. "A Study of the Causes and Consequences of the Economic
Status of Migratory Farm Workers in Illinois, Indiana, Michigan and
Wisconsin, 1940–1958." Ph.D. diss., University of Notre Dame, 1960.

United States Senate, Committee on the Judiciary. *Cuban Refugee Problem.
Hearings Before the Subcommittee to Investigate Problems Connected with
Refugees and Escapees*. Part 2—Grand Rapids, Michigan (14 October 1963).
Washington, D.C.: Government Printing Office, 1963.

United States Senate, Committee on the Judiciary. *Resettlement of Cuban
Refugees*. Washington, D.C.: Government Printing Office, 1964.

Valdes, Dennis N. "*Betabeleros:* The Formation of an Agricultural Proletariat in
the Midwest, 1897–1930." *Labor History* 30 (fall 1989): 536–62.

———. *Al Norte: Agricultural Workers in the Great Lakes Region, 1917–1970*.
Austin: University of Texas Press, 1991.

Valdes, Dionicio N. *Barrios Nortenos: St. Paul and Midwestern Mexican
Communities in the Twentieth Century*. Austin: University of Texas Press,
2000.

Valdez, Margarita, ed. *Tradiciones del Pueblo: Traditions of Three Mexican Feast*

Days in Southwest Detroit. Detroit: Casa de Unidad Cultural Arts and Media Center, 1990.

Vargas, Zaragosa. "Life and Community in the 'Wonderful City of the Magic Motor': Mexican Immigrants in 1920s Detroit." *Michigan Historical Review* 15 (spring 1989): 47–68.

———. *Proletarians of the North: A History of Mexican Industrial Workers in Detroit and the Midwest, 1917–1933.* Berkeley: University of California Press, 1993.

Weeks, John R., and Joseph Spielberg Benitez. "The Cultural Demography of Midwestern Chicano Communities." In *The Chicano Experience.* Edited by Stanley A. West and June Macklin: 229–51. Boulder, Colo.: Westview Press, 1979.

Willson, Kay D. "The Historical Development of Migrant Labor in Michigan Agriculture." Master's thesis, Michigan State University, 1978.

Wilson, Brian. "The Spirit of the Motor City: Three Hundred Years of Religious History in Detroit." *Michigan Historical Review* 27 (spring 2001): 21–56.

Yinger, Winthrop. *Cesar Chavez: The Rhetoric of Nonviolence.* Hicksville, N.Y.: Exposition Press, 1975.

Archival Collections/Research Institutes

Archives of the Archdiocese of Detroit, Detroit, Michigan

Burton Historical Collection, Detroit Public Library

Fort Wayne Diocese Archives, Fort Wayne, Indiana

Julian Samora Research Institute, Michigan State University, East Lansing, Michigan

Redemptorist Archives, Brooklyn, New York

Robert E. Lucey Papers, University of Notre Dame Archives, South Bend Indiana

Walter P. Reuther Library, Wayne State University (United Farm Worker Union Collection and the César Chávez Collection).

Videos

Forjando una Comunidad: A History of Mexicans in Detroit (1999)

Los Repatriados: Exiles from the Promised Land (2001)

References for Latino Music

Bloch, Peter. *La-Le-Lo-Lai: Puerto Rican Music and its Performers.* New York: Plus Ultra, 1973.

Gerard, Charley, and Marty Sheller. *Salsa: The Rhythm of Latin Music.* Crown Point, Ind.: White Cliffs Media Company, 1989.

Pena, Manuel. *The Texas-Mexican Conjunto: History of a Working-Class Music.* Austin: University of Texas Press, 1985.

Roberts, John S. *Black Music of Two Worlds.* New York: Praeger, 1972.

———. *The Latin Tinge: The Impact of Latin American Music on the United States.* New York: Oxford University Press, 1979.

Strachwitz, Chris, ed. *Lydia Mendoza: A Family Autobiography.* Houston: Arte Público Press, 1993.

Index